MW01519751

GO AWAY LITTLE GIRL

...Growing up unwanted

Isha Peralta

Acknowledgements

Many thanks to my sister Barbara Molin, my husband James Peralta and my son Jason Blue for offering to proofread. Your feedback has been most insightful and inspiring.

My deep gratitude goes to God and his angels who made the writing a fairly smooth process. It felt as if God called me to write my story because it flowed. I cried at some parts: the pain, and hurt pouring out on the pages... But I found peace sitting in God's presence while re-examining my childhood.

Printed by KDP

To my beloved grandchildren Cypress, Tristan, Vivienne and Gabrielle:
May your life be rich with wonder, critical thinking and gratitude to God.

Foreword: written to me on March 5, 2013

This is Isha's 'oversoul' here, otherwise known as Guardian Angel UM23.. Time to go out on the limb and test my connection to her. I am filled with trepidation and anxiety as I am far from perfect myself, and she is not an easy protégé. She's all too often insisting on learning things the pain filled way rather than tune-in to the frequency of my guidance and advice. Will she hear and write what my still, small voice guides her to write, or will she allow her ego to dictate? How well will she translate and communicate my lessons?

I think I'm ready to risk living under observation, but is she? Will she make a fool out of me and her other incarnations, or will she display the courage to try and fail and try again until she gets it right?

Stay tuned and if by chance my greatest fears are realized, at least I will take comfort in the possibility that through watching her stumble and fall in her attempt at writing, the reader might be encouraged to more fully explore their own consciousness. After all, it's not difficult to surpass a slow learner like her. That's me: always finding a way to see the glass as half full!

Introduction

We plan, God laughs.

What if unwelcome events that happen <u>to</u> us, actually happen <u>for</u> us? Perhaps for reasons that are so much more important than our physical well being? What if the most important prayer is "God's will, not mine, be done"?

This morning I walked down to the ocean and was dismayed to see more than two dozen people fishing in my favorite, semi-enclosed ocean swimming spot, where I like to do laps. Because it's semi-enclosed, they've come here to catch their bait. These days I am quicker to get over my disappointment, so I made the choice to turn away and walk down the beach. I love to walk the beach but am often too uncomfortable to do it alone. I actually do really well on my own but I still have a strongly ingrained aversion to solitude.

What contradictory human 'doings' we are: there have been so many days, months and years of living inland, when I told myself that I would walk alone more, if only I could do it on a sandy beach, far from car exhaust. But I couldn't, so I didn't. So many of my friends and family love to hike but since I am deathly afraid of wood ticks, that is not an option for me. But now here I am, living three blocks from a beautiful tropical beach and I still often find an excuse to not do it. But my bad knees need the exercise and so I say a quiet 'thank you' as I recognize the presence of the fishermen as a gift, and soon the discomfort of solitude is overcome.

I used to have a beach walking buddy, but the 2020 coronavirus pandemic has put a stop to our new found friendship. She is over 70 and after eight months is still very afraid to venture out. And making new friends in these days of extended lockdowns and social distancing is impossible. On top of that, for the past year I had been looking forward to a summer holiday in my hometown in Poland, but border closures have forced me to cancel my ticket and accommodation bookings. Depression followed. After two months of sleeping the days as well as the nights away, I finally had no choice but to ask God to help me make a new plan. I realized that the solitude inspired ruminations have led me back to writing. 'Trapped' within my condo overlooking the ocean, I actually couldn't design a better environment. I was now able to see that the pandemic happened as a gift for me.

The same way that cancer had been a gift, twenty years earlier.

The mere fact that we are forced to go unconscious for nearly a third of our life, tells me that we are not fully in charge. We can get by without food for several weeks, but we cannot go more than a few days without sleep. And like food, the right amount of sleep is very beneficial but the excess that I was indulging in, was becoming seriously detrimental. Sleep is a powerful force beyond our control. Therefore, there must be something or somewhere very important that awaits us in that state of being.

The triad

The way I see it, our DNA controls a third of our life, our childhood nurturing (or lack of) controls another third, while Fate, Destiny and Karma are in charge of the rest.

How can it be otherwise when it's obvious that each baby displays a unique personality long before they're influenced by the environment that they grow up in? I came to this conclusion having raised three children that were very different right from birth.

I like to imagine (and strongly believe) that before we came into this life, our spirit selves sat around a 'table' and planned our soul journeys to the physical realm. Just like any trip we may be getting ready for, we discuss with those closest to us, things like: who we will stay with, what we would like to achieve and how to get the most benefit from the experience. We decide on what baggage we need to bring with us. And how we will connect and help each other. The goal for our souls on these trips cannot be other than spiritual growth - as no one returns with even one physical possession, though God only knows, the Egyptians have certainly tried!

Then we are born, and by the time we are able to talk in sentences, or within three years, most of us lose the memory of that meeting and the trip itinerary has been misplaced. Soon we no longer spend 12 to 14 hours sleeping and thus disconnect from our place of origin even more.

Then the goal gradually changes as we become more and more physically focused: going to school so that we can get a good job in order to earn enough money to satiate our physical desires. And the purpose of our life's journey - that I am a spiritual being having a human experience - is quickly forgotten.

Dear Father of my Soul,

Open my heart, quiet my mind,

guide my hand

And allow Your inspiration to flow through me.

Protect me from distractions and resistance,

Strengthening my resolve.

Make me Your instrument for wisdom and
peace

And allow my words to bring awareness

and understanding of Your plan,

to make life richer for others.

May I always work in a way

that awakens the awareness of

Your Holy Spirit in others.

Chapter 1 1954 - 1960

"What is to give light, must endure burning"
- Viktor Frankl

If my parents never wanted a baby when they found out that they were expecting me, but couldn't do anything about it, then imagine how unhappy my mother was throughout her pregnancy. Is it possible that this can influence a baby's development in the womb? My parents did not love each other but circumstances forced them together. They had other plans and the war had ruined them.

Then, perhaps they finally came to terms with having another baby and there I was: arrived in this world, BUT not a BOY. So they are disappointed again.

At least with my older sister it was a novelty and only a part time chore as my mother put her into a government nursery and went back to work when my sister was three months old.

But the look in her parents' eyes from then on probably contributed to her view for the duration of her life, as not being wanted, not being accepted, not being loved and not being good enough.

Double that disappointment when my mother was pregnant for the fifth time. Poland was mostly a Catholic country, so any kind of birth control was forbidden. Plus the Party needed lots of future workers. My mother could not face a third illegal abortion and, lo and behold, that's when I took the opportunity to come into the world. You can imagine how it added insult to injury when I, the second daughter arrived. And in my parents' view, there would be nothing that I could ever do to make it up to them.

And what if the greatest gift being offered to us is the one that pushes us out of our comfort zone, the opportunity to live the life that we're most afraid of? In that case, what a perfect set of parents for immeasurable spiritual growth for me!

My mother carried a martyr complex. Her main teaching to me was based on her Romanian ancestral beliefs that people were most vulnerable to evil magic while they were being praised and adored. She therefore concurred and strengthened my father's philosophy on children: never say a kind or encouraging word, give a hug, or indicate anything that could be classified as loving or adoring. That will bring tragedy. In her eyes the world had proven this point of view to her in a most cruel way. She was just 13 in 1939 and being raised by a devout Catholic mother who attended mass every morning, when her mother, baby brother and the family dog were killed in the first week of World War 2 when a bomb fell into their yard. They were the only casualties in the village of Wegrów - a distance of 88 kilometres - where they moved to avoid the dangers of big city Warsaw.

Throughout her life my mother gave me the impression that she was comfortable with rigid structure, sacrifice and self denial. She repressed her feelings and instincts and had trouble feeling at ease in family relationships.

Yet she conceived very easily. What if motherhood was her destiny in order to teach her how to relax, have fun and nurture?

All around in this post war Communist environment of fear and uncertainty, there was much proof of victory over death. After the atrocities they witnessed during WW2, the anticipation and arrival of new life gave most people hope for the future. I saw it all around me growing up: relatives and parents of friends who treasured their babies and children. Whose hearts were still able to love.

My father was a middle child, the second (spare) son of a neglectful merchant father. My father's attempt to earn his father's love by saving him during the war, backfired and he was severely traumatized. This happened when he was still a teenager. He therefore became a proud atheist and nihilist following the philosophy of Arthur Schopenhauer who wrote about the world being filled with endless strife.

My father loved books on psychology and the futility of life as well as endless discussions on very depressing subjects. What's the point of debating whether it's better never to have been born since we are already here and have the option to rediscover our purpose? But he was unmovable in his beliefs. I'm sure that David Benatar's 2008 book "Better Never to Have Been: The Harm of Coming into Existence" would have been one of his favorites. He hated war yet had natural skills to have survived in very difficult circumstances. He was lost in contradictions: he lacked awareness of others' needs, yet couldn't understand why they weren't like him or at least, why they didn't do as he wished. He spent years trying to convert anyone and everyone to his point of view about the hopelessness of life. And so his conclusion was regret at not being able to live his life as a hermit.

But what if he had been open to Destiny's plan for him? Perhaps if he was willing to focus his attention away from himself, become a champion for justice and peace on the behalf of others, he would have gotten more positive results.

My parents met in 1949 through relatives and why they got married is another story. They settled in my father's small home town in southern Poland far from the big city of Warsaw where my mother was raised, and far from her father who stayed in Wegrów with his new wife and baby son. It wasn't difficult for my father to stop her from attending church and espouse his outlook.

As for me, Destiny had its reasons to give me the kind of parents who were too damaged to value children. Dependence and the desire to be taken care of, constituted a large portion of my 'baggage' when I arrived. To be part of a family was my greatest wish and a stable home was where I anticipated finding the greatest comfort.

And so, on June 1st, between the hours of 4:30pm and 5pm Poland time, I arrived. For astrological studies, I've chosen 4:54pm as the precise time.

Now came the question of my name. My mother wanted to call me Isa or Isia, which is a short form of Isabella. My father appeared to agree.

They also agreed that my middle name would be Lidia, after my father's sister. However, when he went to the registry, he registered me as Irena Lidia. Irena was the name of his favorite cousin who was one of the few people that shared his philosophy. My mother was heartbroken when she found out but insisted that I would be Isia in every way but on official documents.

And so I became known as Isia in Poland and Isha in Canada to ease the pronunciation. The name Isha has many meanings in various languages:

In Hebrew it means 'woman'
In Arabic it means 'night prayer'
In Hindu it means 'protector'
In Sanskrit it means 'goddess - one who looks after'
In Japanese it means 'doctor'
And in American Indian Ishani or Ishana means desirable.

My mother chose well and I've always been happy with my name and strived to live up to it. Though my parents never used them, I've loved my name's diminutive forms (or hypocorisms) even more; Isienka, Isiunia and Isiuvna. They convey a sense of affection, intimacy or endearment and perhaps that's why they still warm my heart like nothing else.

My older sister Basia mostly saw me as unwelcome competition in the environment of scarcity of love, approval and acceptance. Being three and a half years older and remembering life without competition for the crumbs of love and affection that used to be solely hers, she resented my intrusion. June 1st, Children's Day, was chosen by many countries after the war, when brand new citizens were celebrated. Children were given gifts, then dressed up and taken for ice cream and cake slices at the bakeries around town. It was the most special day, second only to Christmas. From future proof, I'm sure my parents were not disappointed to have that obligation merged with a birthday. That year, my grandmother likely took my sister on the rounds. But having been handed to a nursery from a very young age, I don't doubt that she resented yet another infringement on her sparse time with them.

Perhaps she felt that her survival depended on everything being in order according to her view of how others ought to behave so that she could relax and trust?

What if she had been given encouragement that the plan that Destiny had for her was better than her plan, and that things were unfolding properly, regardless of how it seemed? Had she been influenced to connect and trust a Higher Power, perhaps she would have been able to accept that my arrival had the potential to contribute to her advantage and therefore her greater happiness. But she wasn't and so it didn't.

Now you get the picture of how suitable this 'classroom' was for a highly sensitive and cheerful soul. One who soon forgot why she chose this family…

Not having recovered from the horrors of war, I annoyed and irritated my father to no end with my cheerful nature. Having felt betrayed, he, unlike relatives and neighbors whose dependence on God was increased by similar ordeals, needed to deny any semblance of faith, hope, the miracle of life, and the simplicity and joy of innocence.

His attitude was so different from what I witnessed around me: people their age, having lived through the war, cherished their children and had a deep sense of commitment to making their lives better. I saw many sacrifices made for the younger generation. My family stood out, as our parents had nothing but resentment towards us and their peers noticed it and thought it was odd.

But perhaps my mother's connection to the

church's teachings was stronger than she could control, for she risked the wrath of her husband for it. Years later, the downstairs neighbor told me that she went with my mother - who swore her to secrecy - when she took me to be christened.

To my father, I was a burden, a detriment and an inconvenience and for 58 years, he took every opportunity to remind me. A female who was a constant, irritating contradiction to his belief in the superiority of males, the absence of God, and the futility of life. Wanting simply to love and be loved, I did everything wrong, starting with the unforgivable: I was born. Adding insult to injury, I was not a boy. Third strike against me, they already had one unwanted girl: the novelty bond, however thin, had been allocated. I was thrust into their care against their will. He couldn't blame a God that he didn't believe in so instead, he never forgave his wife and daughters for depriving him of his dream life. As for me, my life could never be the one that my all too human nature couldn't help but crave: the ordinary life of an ordinary, wanted child.

It is very difficult to get past the feeling of not being loved by one's parents and my mortal mind could not accept it. Or perhaps I was aided in the process of letting go because in order to cope, I convinced myself that I was adopted. It was my very first secret. I needed to believe that. In my heart there was no other explanation for the lack of affection that I experienced. It was inconceivable to me how parents could not cherish their baby. I saw it all around me: hugs, indulgence, loving reprimands, devotion. Obviously then it wasn't their fault: they could not love me as their own, because I wasn't. I felt validated when people told me that I looked nothing like my family.

When I eventually shared these secrets with my mother, she burst my bubble by telling me that mine was a home birth. She made the decision due to the fact that at the time my sister was born, there was a case of babies being switched at the local hospital. I can understand how her relief contributed to her ability to bond with her firstborn. My birth however did not push any primal buttons of protection and years later, hypnosis confirmed what I already knew: my birth was not a day for celebration.

In the mid 1950's it was still a very respectable vocation for a woman to be a stay at home mother, so due to my birth, my mother kept my sister at home for the next 3 years as well. But I imagine that being a baby, I was the main focus and that greatly increased my sister's animosity.

We are all broken: that's how the light gets in
- Ernest Hemingway

Already resenting having to share her parents with me, my sister was frequently saddled with my care and she took delight in tormenting me by passing down the rejection that she felt - while I looked up to her: I wanted to be just like her. Being dressed alike was my greatest joy and her greatest misery. (funny, in our middle-age years when people asked if we were twins, it was my misery and her joy to hear it)

I have memories of the bruises that my sister left by doing what was called a Chinese burn. She would place her hands around my forearm and twist in different directions.

Painful.

Very painful.

That and the abandonment that I experienced the many times she ran away leaving me behind was more tragic to this 4-5 year old than parental neglect. Sharing a home devoid of nurturing, I had placed her in the role of my ally but to her life as to our parents', I was a detriment rather than a gift.

Though she was twice my age and size, my parents refused to intercede, claiming that that's just what siblings do.

This memory influenced my future parenting to a significant degree. The sibling relationship is not equal in these early years and it's wrong to think that the younger one can 'fend for themselves' or is equally to blame for any conflict. Four years is a huge difference at this age and parents must protect the younger child.

Left to fend for myself and unable to protect myself physically, at the age of 4 or 5, I resourcefully learned that I could fight back by developing a sharp tongue.

I don't have much other knowledge of the early years at home with my mother and sister before I entered two years of kindergarten at the age of five. My mother's recollections whenever I asked, always left me feeling shamed and rejected. Except for our summers at the Baltic seaside town of Sopot, to her it was a time best forgotten she said. Those summers were the only time that I remember her laughter. It's like she came alive when she was away from her unemotional husband's disapproval and actually able to show a semblance of love to my sister and I.

I remember being three, four and five, and my father leaving the house to go to the train station to buy advance tickets for us. Then he'd come home and it would be a mad rush to get back to the station in time for the train. Once there, my sister and mother would barely board and he would then pass me to my mother as the train was pulling out of the station. We took the eight hour long steam train ride there and back, and I slept in a little hammock strung between the overhead baggage shelves.

Some of my favourite times spent with my mother were the many, many days playing at the beach in Sopot. On windy days each family would set up a windbreak around their blanket. At lunch, she would ask another mother to watch us while she returned to our little rented flat to cook. Then she would come to get us and after lunch the three of us would all nap. On rainy days she would play cards with us.

Sometimes our father joined us for part of the time. On occasion, he would rent a kayak and paddle us around close to shore. My mother was already deathly afraid of water as he once pushed her into a swimming pool on a 'sink or swim' lesson. He just could not understand or accept why she wasn't willing to be more like him.

I also remember visiting her father Jan, stepmother Maria and half brother Andrzej on their orchard in Wegrów, an hour outside of Warsaw. Actually, my very first clear memory at the age of three was confirmed by my mother. I remember being laid down for a nap on the big straw filled mattress and goose down quilt and watching the flies buzzing around. Perhaps I slept. Suddenly, the rare sound of an engine got my full attention. My mother's cousin came by on a motorcycle. I ran outside very excited and begged to sit on it. My uncle Tofek offered to take me for a short ride. My mother did not object but my sister quickly insisted on being included. She was put on the back seat while I sat on the fuel tank.

Uncle Tofek took us on a dirt road where we saw a gypsy camp across a field. There was music and we could see them dancing. I remember the painted wagons and the sound of the tambourines. This was an amazingly happy moment for me and I was always grateful that my mother allowed it. It also was the beginning of my love of motorcycles.

She took a stand against my father twice. The first time she found out that he'd been going for coffee with some woman in town while we were very young. She told him if it happened again, she would take us and leave. The second time I was

26

maybe five and he hit me. She told him not to ever do that again and amazingly he never again physically hurt us.

Here was her Guardian Angel confirming to her that when she shared her feelings she won.

My home was called 'Pajta'

My hometown was called Cieszyn, which loosely meant 'to be happy'. It was established in the year 810 and is one of the oldest towns in Silesia. According to legend, three sons of a Slav king – Bolko, Leszko and Cieszko, met near a spring after long solitary pilgrimages, and in their happiness at being reunited decided to found a new settlement. The population in the 1950's was around 30,000.

We lived at Plac Koscielny #3, in a rented 400 square foot apartment in an old Lutheran school house built in 1725 that had been converted into living spaces in 1904. My grandmother's apartment where she raised my father and his two siblings was across the hall from us. Our second floor windows looked out onto the Lutheran church. The lavatories at the end of the shared hallways consisted of holes cut into wooden benches with a holding tank below in the backyard. Our apartment was half of an old classroom: cramped accommodation for four people and so, life was best lived outdoors whenever weather permitted it.

Each apartment was heated by a tile furnace that burned coal. This was the only source of heat in the winter and ours was in the bathroom, which was strange, as that was the room we spent the least amount of time in. Wall rugs were hung on walls by the beds. Each apartment also had a tap for cold running water. If hot was needed, it had to be heated on the stove.

The old church school building was filled with other families and on warm weather days, the women congregated outside to sit in groups and peel potatoes, knit or darn socks, keep an eye on the children and gossip. The joy filled camaraderie and unrefined local dialect offended my mother's Warsaw upbringing. She refused to interact with them and was horrified whenever I picked up the lingo. I also loved the sound of the church bells coming from across the street, telling everyone what time it was, whereas they annoyed her. I started to learn that I could get approval with my silence.

When I was four, my father's sister Lidia arrived with her husband, her son Jurek and their dog Kazan for a visit. As this was in December, ten year old Jurek accompanied St. Nicholas on the 6th, walking like a midget and dressed as a devil. He was distributing dry sticks and pieces of coal as a warning to children whose behavior needed improvement if they wanted to receive a gift at Christmas. This memory sticks in my mind, as I was terrified.

My father's mother Ewa had been born in 1899 on the currently Czech side of the river in a small village called Łyżbice, when the region was still a part of the Austro-Hungarian Empire. She spoke fluent German, Polish and Czech as well as the dialect. She was devoted to keeping in touch with her extended family. Since both her and my grandfather's ancestors came from the Czech side, she often crossed the border to visit them. Her husband's grandmother Zuzanna Sikora had four sisters and many descendants who lived nearby, and my grandmother corresponded with them all. One of the sisters named Kasia married into the Śliwka family but since being widowed, she lived below us. My grandmother, as well as my cousin's mother whose grandmother Maria was Kasia's sister as well, looked after her.

My grandmother or Babusia, as everyone called her, was a quiet, intelligent and serious working woman who dressed impeccably. Her hair was down to her waist and she always wore it in a braided bun. She taught me how to make cards for Mother's Day and I loved to practice writing letters under her guidance. She was proud of my penmanship. There were nights that I slept over and she continued to teach me to say my prayers before bed. She sang to me and the song I remember is *"Kiedy Ranne Wstają Zorze"*. Then I would pick out different shapes in the ceiling until I dropped off to sleep.

She had a baby grand piano that my sister and I learned to play. We began by taking lessons at the convent in town. We both loved learning there and were even taught to play several duets. I remember my grandmother also had one of the first telephones.

My Babusia's love was supplemented by other people in my life that took joy in my presence. For the most part, I felt valued and welcomed. I didn't really notice that my parents took very little interest in me.

Chapter 2 - 1961

It was January and a new year started. I was in my second year of kindergarten at #1 Chrobrego St. It is still there. At the entrance, we had our hooks and cupboards identified by a little picture of an animal, bird or insect. Mine was a ladybug.

I remember going to the brick factory on a field trip and making a hedgehog out of toothpicks and clay when we got back. I remember compulsory nap time where each of us had a little bed with a chair in front.

I remember how calm the teacher in our class was when a boy - Dzinek Gelen - a rascal by nature, was trying to show off by climbing up and walking on the bannister on the second floor just outside our room. She calmly talked him down.

I met my lifelong friends in kindergarten. There was Jadzia, Halinka, Czesia, Hania, Jola, Waldek and Janusz. But my closest friend's name was Danusia and she was also my third cousin. She lived in the church parish house across the square from us.

But most of all I remember the joy of us performing the 'Krakowiak', a Polish folk dance. I decided then and there that I wanted to be a professional folk dancer when I grew up.

I loved school and kindergarten holds some of my favorite memories. I remember an orderly, strict and loving environment. We were indoctrinated into becoming model citizens. Love and loyalty to the motherland was strongly instilled. Family was of secondary importance therefore growing up in a communist country was very beneficial for many children, whether they came from an exceptionally poor or an alcoholic home.

In the afternoons my mother or grandmother would come to pick me up and I would then spend an hour or two finding things to quietly occupy myself with, in the music store/ instrument repair shop 'Ton' and the adjacent office where they both worked. Sometimes my sister Basia and I would be sent to the bakery and dessert shop three doors down and our favorite treat there was a whipping cream horn. If bread was bought, I loved the soft middle while my sister loved the ends. I remember using stale bread to clean the office walls.

The third person and manager in that office was Pan Krupa and he was in love with my grandmother. Even though she was a widow, I didn't notice her returning his attention. He was however, often included in family celebrations that she hosted.

My aunt Lidia arrived again and arranged to have a washing machine delivered as well as a modern toilet installed in her apartment so her mother wouldn't have to go down the hall to the communal ones. What a luxury it was to own her very own toilet. And I also remember using newspaper strips to wipe!

I remember that Aunt Lidia brought me legos. I also had a metal circuit toy, a metal car track and a shelf full of books. My favourite was *'Bajarka Opowiada'*: a book of fairytales that I inherited from Basia after she grew out of it.

My grandmother still had a coal stove and a coal tile furnace like we did. And she had an iron that was heated with a rock being placed inside it.

The summer was spent in the huge front and back yards, making tents by clipping blankets to the clotheslines and anchoring them with bricks. Kicking a ball on the grass. Climbing the apple trees. Raiding the vegetable gardens, eating rhubarb and gooseberries and apples. There was also one very old and very tall pear tree. There were chicken coops and rabbit cages in the backyard. We would feed the rabbits dandelion leaves and watch one or two get killed and skinned for Sunday dinner. We would crawl into the chicken coops and persuade the youngest boys to show us their secrets. My grandmother, like most of the neighbors, had a vegetable garden plot, but my parents did not. My father had no interest in raising any chickens or rabbits either so we rarely had meat. But occasionally he would purchase a skinned rabbit from one of the neighbors.

Having the memory of bacon bits on our boiled potatoes or sucking the marrow out of a bone makes me think that this was a rare treat. Duck or goose was difficult to get unless you had family that lived on a farm - which we did not - or you were a doctor like my father's psychiatrist brother, whose patients sometimes paid him in poultry or ham.

We spent much time sitting on the curb watching weddings and funerals going in and out of the nearby church. We learned to distinguish the meaning of the color of the feathers on the horses' headpieces and how many horse drawn carriages there were. After the service the church bells would ring and people would walk behind the carriages to the hall or to the cemetery.

Other times we ran across the street to the park which was next to the church. It consisted of tall grass with neglected lilac bushes on one side, where we would explore. I also remember the snowberry bushes there with the white berries that were fun to pop. There were benches, a sandbox and swings and for us children this was the nicest place in the world. On occasion the carnival would set up there, and what I remember most was the merry-go-round that had suspended swings.

There were seven of us: Małgosia and her sister Ala who lived below my grandmother, Bambo and Jura who lived upstairs in the end unit. Leszek who lived below us and a boy who lived upstairs beside us. I was the oldest of our group. Most of our friends were siblings of our sibling. My sister had Heniek who was Małgosia's brother and Ewa who was Bambo's sister to play with but she preferred to read and rarely participated by then.

Thank goodness that we lived in housing that was fenced and filled with warm hearted people who watched over me. Though my sister and I shared a small bedroom, my parents made it clear that their peace was not to be disturbed indoors. Rain or shine, summer or winter, apart from school hours, I was dressed and sent outside from after breakfast until sundown to play in the fenced front and rear gardens or in hallways and staircases if the weather was too harsh.

When the grass was scythed and piled for burning, we ran home to get potatoes and salt, and waited eagerly for the flames to go out. Then we buried our potatoes in the ashes. What rejoicing there was as our faces were covered in soot!

School

The schoolyard was adjacent to our backyard, separated first by a wooden fence later followed by a chain link fence. Rather than walking around, we made a convenient hole to shorten our walk.

There was a bunker with two exits in the schoolyard leftover from WW2. Even though they were filled with broken debris and dirt and stank of urine, older girls and boys went in there to smoke and kiss.

I turned seven and it was the age for all children to start school. We were given 4 vaccinations: DTP (Diphtheria, Tetanus, Pertussis) Smallpox, Polio and Tuberculosis. We were allotted two uniforms each. A black button down, shiny shirt dress with a white, starched, snapped-on collar for the girls and black shirts with white collars for the boys. There was always a handkerchief in our pockets and our leather shoes were always polished. The only day that we were out of uniform, was picture day at the end of the school year. It was wonderful not to have to decide what to wear each day, and there was no jealousy or income level obvious to cause bullying. At school we were taught that we were all equal, no matter what family we came from. Introverts were valued and respected. Extroverts were frowned upon.

Pani Nakielna was our grade one teacher and there were 40 of us. We all loved her. We sat two to a desk in long wooden desks where the top lifted up, with the benches attached. We each had a set of coloured pencils, an inkwell and a nib pen which had the tip made of metal and the holder made of wood. Each lesson in our writing books ended with a strip of decoration that we ourselves designed. The main book that we learned from was 'Elementarz'. Primer. It was beautiful, filled with pictures, stories and poems. I still have a copy.

My cousin Danusia and I shared a front row desk. We encouraged each other to excel through friendly competition. As my classmates have told me recently at our 50th reunion, I was remembered as the best reader in our class.

Besides learning arithmetic, basic geography, reading and writing, these early classes also included instruction in ballroom dancing, embroidery and darning socks. The classroom was so quiet you could actually hear a pin drop. This was normal in every classroom, as we only spoke when the teacher asked us a question. There was rarely a discipline problem.

After school I stayed in the cafeteria where we were fed lunch and did homework. Most often we got some kind of potato dumplings with sauce. I would stay there until my parents got home. I was then allowed into our apartment only to change out of my uniform and take off my shoes before I went outside barefooted to play until dark. Shoes were difficult to come by and were rarely worn apart from school, walks with parents and posing for pictures.

What we ate

The fall brought the winter deliveries. Each family got an allotment of potatoes and an allotment of coal. Both went into their own basement cubicles. It was my father's job to fetch the coal for the tile furnace that stood in the bathroom, and it was the childrens' job to fetch potatoes and peel them for dinner each day.

For that, we needed a flashlight and some friends as there were rats to be reckoned with.

As well as coal and potatoes, a large amount of cabbage was acquired. Sauerkraut was a necessary winter staple and us children were put to work. While my grandmother and mother chopped, my sister and I stomped the salted chopped cabbage with our bare feet in a large wooden tub. Then it was put into a large ceramic crock and covered with a clean cloth, a wooden circular plank weighed down by a heavy stone. The crock was kept on the attic stairs next to us. As long as it's kept submerged in salt water, sauerkraut can last over two years without refrigeration.

There was also a slop bucket there for a woman who owned a pig. In return, she brought us a sausage at Christmas.

Cabbage, potatoes, onions and beets were the vegetables that sustained us over the winter. Occasionally there were pickles and carrots and kohlrabi. But fresh bread was the most important item and each family was entitled to it. As with eggs and milk, this was easily available and the responsibility of children to fetch. As with the potato trips to the basement, my friends and I fulfilled these tasks in small groups of three or four. The store that sold eggs and milk was up the hill at the end of the block. It never ceased to entertain us how each egg was held up to a lightbulb to make sure there was no baby chick inside. Then they were placed in a paper bag for us to carry home along with the milk filled aluminum canister that each family had specifically for that purpose. We may have been six or seven, but we were necessary to the efficient running of the family.

The bakeries were a bit further. So when I was seven and if bread was needed very early for breakfast, I'd see who was available and we would run down to the commercial bakery that opened at 5a.m. By the time we got there, there was usually a short line. Watching it come piping hot out of the ovens with that heavenly aroma, was also a treat.

Bread was a staple of post war Polish life. A rye bread unlike any other outside our region, it was a meal in itself. They said that the secret ingredient that could not be copied elsewhere, was our local water. Clean and pure. This bread was given to me as a child slathered in salted goose fat called *smalec*. If there was no *smalec*, we got onions on butter sprinkled with salt, while Malgosia and Ala's mother sprinkled theirs with sugar. If there happened to be jam, we got jam, but without butter. One or the other, not both.

My town of Cieszyn is still famous for 'kanapki': an artistically arranged open faced sandwich consisting of slightly stale white bread spread with butter and topped as high as would hold with small thin slices of egg, sardines, cheese, a bit of ham or sausage if available, tomato and even pickle.

"Despite ever changing culinary habits and the fashion for big nutritious satisfying sandwiches, the tradition of open sandwiches has been preserved by the city of Cieszyn. For several decades now, a crucial part of the city's culinary landscape has been the open herring sandwich, and it even has its own festival. Available in almost every convenience store, it's made up of a slice of bread, mayonnaise, herring, hard-boiled egg and chopped parsley. Although the ingredients are not very sophisticated, the taste is said to be difficult to replicate."

- Magdalena Kasprzyk

The other place to buy freshly made bread was a bakery store several blocks away in the opposite direction to the milk store and across from the newsstand which was called a kiosk.

The kiosk was an especially favorite destination for us and we were happy to be sent on an errand for the newspaper. Ruch newsagent kiosks have been a feature on Polish streets since 1918 and besides newspapers and magazines, sold cigarettes, matches, cheap little toys and penny candy. No trip was complete without a treat as payment for our services.

The rest of the shopping required waiting for hours in long lines for hard to get and often rationed products, and that was left to the adults. Retirement kicked in at age 60, so most grandparents were needed to take charge of the shopping as no one had fridges and food had to be sought almost daily. Besides that they also took care of the cooking, childcare and home maintenance. It was also easier for them to cross the border bridge over to the Czech side where more products were available, especially if, like my grandmother, they still had family there. I remember she took me with her once to visit some extended family called Walach. They had two boys a few years older than me, and the one who was about fourteen, was especially kind.

As a small child, I remember getting a soft boiled egg or hot semolina porridge called '*grysik*' (the hard grains left after the milling of flour) for breakfast, while my parents ate open faced sandwiches and drank tea or on occasion '*Inka*', which was a chicory coffee substitute. Tea was the most popular drink as coffee was not available. The tea leaves were brewed in a teapot to make '*esencia*', a strong tea base to which hot water was added and which was then served in a glass placed inside a metal holder. One teapot containing the equivalent of one teabag's loose tea, usually lasted the average family for the whole day's meals. Polish people drank very weak tea.

The food I remember eating most was boiled potatoes with chives and buttermilk to drink (*maślanka*). Potatoes were prepared in a vast variety of other ways as well, so they rarely got boring. *Kopytka, knedle*: potato dough dumplings filled with plums, sprinkled with butter and sugar. Potato pancakes, potato *pyzy*. And of course the best vodka for the adults was made from potatoes. On a visit years later, I was told that Poland was famous for its 17 varieties of potatoes. As an example, in Sweden the brands were labelled in the store whereas in Poland there was only one basket with the mixture and labelled 'potatoes'. A person had no choice as far as what kind of potatoes they were buying.

I remember the case was the same with hard cheese. The only choice was between white cheese and yellow cheese. This remained the case well into the 1990's.

Other foods we ate were cabbage rolls, *bigos* and *mizeria* which is a cucumber salad. Pickle soup and mushroom soup. Tripe soup (*flaczki*) made from the stomach lining of a sheep or cow. It sounds disgusting but necessity is the mother of invention and Polish cooks were amazing at creating delicious meals out of nothing. Chicken soup made from feet and beaks with raw egg slowly dropped into the hot broth with added bits of chopped chicken liver, kidney and heart. Cottage cheese with chopped radishes. On occasion there was rice with butter and sugar.

Basia and I only hated one thing: the boiled milk which usually had a slimy 'skin' on top. We were eventually allowed to drink the weak tea instead. And sometimes my father brought home a glass soda water syphon, which carbonated the water and was combined with the raspberry syrup that my grandmother made each fall. I don't remember ever drinking plain water!

The raspberry syrup provided us with vitamin C for the winter months. My Babusia also believed in the medicinal properties of garlic. I don't recall her ever being sick. Another neighbour regularly collected the stinging nettle to treat her arthritis.

Some of the raw milk was poured into glasses and set in the cupboard for a few days to turn sour, making it into something similar to yoghurt. Soured milk (*zsiadłe mleko*) was eaten with a spoon and it was absolutely delicious. Before you scroll down with disgust on your face, wondering why would anyone eat spoiled milk, hear me out. Soured milk can only be made with raw milk. Due to the naturally occurring fermentation process, the sweet flavour turns sour and the milk splits into layers of curd and whey. Additionally if the moisture is squeezed out, it turns into *twaróg,* which is similar to cottage cheese.

For dessert there would be apple or plum *kołocz,* or *naleśniki* with *twaróg* or jam. I remember my sister was quite thin and would take a long time to finish her meal and usually someone had to sit with her and urge her to eat. I think that was her way of getting some much needed attention. I, on the other hand, couldn't finish fast enough and head back outside to play.

Sometimes my mother rewarded me with my favorite treat called *kogel mogel.* She would separate a raw egg and whip the yolk and a teaspoon of sugar in my child ceramic mug. If she was feeling extra generous, she would whip the egg white as well, adding in a bit of cocoa and placing it on top. Eventually she decided that I was old enough to learn how to make it myself and on my first attempt I beat that egg yolk so vigorously, that the bottom of my precious mug broke off. I think that was my first lesson in letting go of material possessions. There were many more to come.

We were also given a daily tablespoon of cod liver oil. As for vitamin D, babies and children were put outside as much as possible.

People rarely moved and when children got married, they frequently lived with one set of parents or the other. Three generations didn't always get along and when within a few years construction began on soviet style apartment blocks just outside of town, independence increased and unavoidable family conflicts were eased.

To ease the tension at home, my mother slept on a cot in the storage area which also served as our closet and my father's darkroom. My father had the living room as his bedroom and we were rarely allowed there. My sister and I shared the small bedroom with furniture that my father had built. We each had a desk and a bank of shelves along the wall and simple couches with slat extensions at the head and foot that when pulled out, were long enough to sleep on as we grew. Looking back, my father had a keen interest in convertible furniture making that lasted for the rest of his life. But carpentry was considered a menial job, not suitable for his status as a university graduate.

Chapter 3   - 1962

We attended school like adults went to work: six days a week with only Sundays off. School was from 8am to 1pm, Adults usually worked from 6-7am until 2-3pm.

Girls' hair had to be either short or tied in two braids. Wearing one braid was a rite of passage into highschool. Often wide ribbons were tied into a large bow. I loved being one of the five girls in our class with long hair. The problem was that Lucek Picha, who sat behind me, would dip my braids into his inkwell. My father's solution was to take me to his barber where my hair was cut short. This was my second experience with letting go. Though I suspect it didn't take and caused my attachment to long hair instead. What I did start to learn was not to take my problems to him, nor accept his solutions.

When the snow fell we were eager to head outside after school and on Sundays. We built snow forts and caves. We sledded. We all seemed to have skis and there was a steep street next to our home that had no horse and wagon traffic in the winter and was a great learning spot. When we had more time, we often trekked to Cieślarówka, which was a longer hill designated for skiing. This was about a kilometre away, so a 20-25 minute walk for our small seven and eight year old feet. There was no lift of any kind. In order to ski down, we had to trudge up. I don't remember any parents coming.

My father's hobby was photography. How different it was back then! Hardly anyone had a camera, and having a family portrait taken at the photo studio was a very formal, expensive and special occasion. Our small apartment had a small narrow room for storage and my father had set up a red light bulb along with his trays and chemicals. There he would do the developing of the black and white pictures he had taken. Sometimes he let us watch him in this 'darkroom'.

He would also take us to the library and instilled a love of books in my sister and me. He also encouraged us in stamp collecting and playing chess. Being prompted, I wrote letters to my cousin Jurek in Canada in the hope of receiving replies with the much coveted foreign stamps.

Some Sundays he would send my sister to the train depot to buy tickets ahead of time. We always seemed to leave the house at the last minute and we would have to run to make it on time. We would take the train for a day trip into the mountains where we would cross-country ski in winter and hike in summer, from one train station to the next with a stop at a lodge for lunch. While there was food for sale there, I only remember eating sandwiches brought from home. Like many families, we also went mushroom picking. On several occasions my father would take my sister to Zakopane where there were ski lifts, for some real downhill skiing. So I guess she did get some privileges based on age.

One day my father brought a dog home. It was a terrier and quite a novelty, as dogs were considered working farm animals who lived outside and ate scraps. It didn't seem to occur to anyone to keep a dog in a town apartment or house. Several weeks later, the dog was gone without an explanation. Years later, I learned from my cousin Magda that she remembers being heartbroken as their terrier had been missing for a period of time. Hmm: adults do strange things.

My birthday came and I woke up to candles on the cake that my mother had baked for me. This is one of the precious memories I have. I think this was the year I received my first piece of 'jewelry'. It was a plastic brooch of a terrier.

Summer was on its way again and at the end of grade one, I was the top student in the class and received a book.

We continued to run errands in packs and stood in line in packs as well: be it for early morning bread or milk. We battled rats in the cellars when we were sent for potatoes. We raided the vegetable gardens and berry bushes. Once again we watched weddings, funerals and the routine of butchering.

Each additional summer meant more glorious freedom. Not only did this communist small town childhood allow us the freedom from parental supervision in the front and back yards, by the time I was eight my friends and I were able to venture further into the town that we lived in. Hania and Jola were added to my friendship with Danusia who lived across the church square. They lived in the same building at the end of the street and we were in the same class. Cars were rare on the cobblestone streets and the only cautions we were given were to stay out of stinging nettle patches, and don't get seduced by the occasional gypsy wagons that passed through and were rumoured to kidnap children. In fact, the only time a child was injured was when Jura's mother tripped and a pot of boiling water poured on his back when he was four years old.

Otherwise I did not know a child with even a broken bone. We were careful as our survival instincts increased with our independence.

Games

Nowadays it's rare to see children running around the neighborhood or even in their own backyard. Since the 1990's, a child without an adult nearby is cause for great concern and perhaps a call to the police department or child welfare services. It's hard to believe that I grew up in exceptional times of glorious freedom and independence. Except for meals and homework, we children spent very little time indoors or with our parents. Parents were not required to play with children as they are today. If we were lucky, they taught us to read or knit as our parents did, but most of the time children were used as extra helping hands around the house so we never dared to say that 'we were bored'! I don't think I even knew the word growing up.

What freedom and camaraderie I enjoyed as I continued my friendship with the neighbourhood gang! With precious little in the way of toys, we were always able to find something to do. We once again climbed trees, roofs, explored alleys and buildings and shared whatever we had: be it a rare bicycle or a single roller skate, candy or a knife. We snuck into the attic and explored among the cobwebs and old furniture.

Each of us was able to get a small knife from home which was our prized possession. Besides sharpening sticks, we used them to play a throwing game that included picking up small stones. We made slings and bows and arrows out of twigs and twine as we played Cowboys and Indians.

I always chose to be an Indian: there was some strong affinity that I felt there. Any stories or books or shows on the subject made me cry with compassion for them. As I gained more exposure to the subject, a strong bond with the Navajo became apparent. Anytime I saw a western, I could quickly identify whether the Navajo tribe was being portrayed. Over the years I had an urge to travel to their lands. When I finally made it to Arizona in 2017, I felt an indescribable kinship there. Whether in a restaurant, a store or on a tour, it felt like I was among my people, like I was home.

We were one pack of boys and girls together. We built more blanket tents on the clotheslines and told stories and read books there. A ball and a skipping rope was something which everyone could afford. Besides those, none of us had any outside toys so we got really good at improvising. What replaced the unavailable merchandise? Sticks, stones, string, newspaper, empty containers, bottles and match boxes. And we cut up old bicycle tires into elastic bands which we used to tie together. A dozen pieces of rubber and we had fun jumping for half a day.

The boys from my school often organized a game of soccer on the cement schoolyard next to our backyard, while we watched from the fence. Often we would retrieve a ball that was kicked into our yard, except when I saw Waldek coming to get it. Then I would wait until he was in our yard and then I would hand him the ball. We never spoke, but it was amazing how often he was the one eager to fetch it.

In the summer we walked to the nearby 'lasek' which was like a small forest with hills and streams, leftover war bunkers and our one public pool. That is where Ewa, Bambo's sister often took us younger children, and where I learned to swim on a leaky inner tube. I had it around my waist and it was only when one of my friends pointed it out to me, that I realized the tube no longer had any air left and I was actually swimming. No one got lost or drowned on these excursions and none of the parents experienced the slightest concern. This little forest ended at the river Olza which was the border with Czechoslovakia. No one was allowed on the river at the risk of getting shot by the border guards.

We picked flowers and stretched blankets on a patch of tall grass and made head wreaths by braiding dandelions or wild daisies. On occasion we stumbled into a patch of stinging nettle and got a temporary red burning rash which we laughed off.

When it was raining or it was too cold outside we stretched blankets on the inside staircase where we played cards or pick-up sticks. We made little animals and people with chestnuts and acorns that we had gathered earlier. The girls were building cardboard dollhouses and pieces of furniture with empty matchboxes, while the boys built pistols, cars and trains. We collected postcards, postage stamps, colorful foil squares, and pebbles. We made sailboats, airplanes and hats out of newsprint.

We played a tracking game where one group left clues made with stick arrows or on bits of paper placed under rocks and the other group had to find them. Another game was 'Countries' where we drew a large portioned off circle in the dirt and then one person would throw a stick up in the air and call out another's name while we ran. That person then had to get the stick and yell 'stop'. Then they would throw the stick at the closest person. If it touched them, the thrower would add a portion of that person's 'country' to their own. If it didn't, then the runner would.

In my childhood we were never bored nor did we question what to play because we knew dozens of various games and activities that did not require any special props apart from those easily found. We spent hours running up and down the church semi circular steps starting from the top along the first step, to the next step, down the length of it, to the next step all the way to the top and back down.

Back in the yard, I remember one time we pooled our money together and rented a bicycle for a day. Another time someone had one rollerskate and we took turns riding on it down the path from the church to our stairs. A person's status was a measure of how good he was at obtaining things to share, not how much he was able to take and hoard.

Near the entrance to the house were stairs with high, wide stone sides. It was our favourite place to sit in the evenings. Ideas for future fun were born there. When dusk arrived, it was time for a game of hide and seek. And thus we played until late evening when our parents started shouting from the windows to call us home.

In the fall we once again buried potatoes in the burning embers of the leaf and grass piles and covered our faces with soot and salt eating them.

It was what many would consider a poor childhood, but it was exciting and peaceful. Nobody valued someone for what toys or games they had, only if they were a nice playmate. And most importantly, while our parents worked at their job and at home, we developed independence by supervising ourselves.

Church

Though my parents had no use for religion, I did. My best friend Małgosia who lived downstairs had a father who was a projectionist at the only cinema in town. He allowed our building's children to see the Sunday matinee for free, if we went to mass first. Church fascinated me especially because my father was so opposed to it.

And since TV hadn't reached us yet, how could I refuse the price of admission to the magic of movies?

Since my father was a strong atheist, I cannot figure out how I got to attend bible classes, but then, being the second girl, my father didn't take much interest in me. Once he found out though, and much to his dismay, he couldn't stop me from attending and I remember vividly being grilled after each class with things like: "if God was all powerful, could he create a rock that was too heavy for Him to lift?" I was forced to listen to many of these 'discussions', which really were monologues and lectures but for an 8-10 year old, that was at least some form of attention. I doubt my father ever realized that I was also attending mass; he thought he had it covered as he forbade his mother from ever taking us along to church and she, like all oppressed women, abided by his wishes.

Surprisingly, she was allowed to take me to the family plot at the Lutheran cemetery. There I would help her pull weeds and pump water for the flowers. It was a serene place with shade and birdsong and I loved going.

I was realizing that something in me was stirring to rebel. I just couldn't resist the awakening spirit within me. I was eight, standing alone in my room having just gotten dressed, when I had this intense awareness of being inside the shell of my body. I was conscious of a blissful spiritual connection while at the same time realizing that just as I had put on my clothes, I was also 'dressed' in my body. How easily that conclusion came to me. This fuelled my spiritual development and encouraged me to remember that I was the driver of my 'vehicle'.

Traumas

Perhaps it was because by the age of eight, I had already had numerous dental procedures. My parents had little interest in dental care and I burdened them with many problems. Toothbrushes were unknown in our house. Cavities were filled and teeth were pulled when needed, but without the benefit of sedation. This has been confirmed by my cousins and classmates who also had their own first hand knowledge. I was restrained and traumatized this way several times in my childhood. My only option was to detach from my body, float up to the ceiling and observe.

Grade two meant a new teacher and her name was Pani Marosz. The two things that I remember was that she would hit my hand with a ruler in order to force me to stop being left handed. I wonder whether I lost my creativity along with my beautiful lettering?

The other thing was that we would have unexpected nail and hand inspections where the principal would arrive at the door and check everyone. Seeing as we played outside at recess and the infraction meant it would get written in the personal book that was kept on us, I along with others, learned how to quickly pick our nails short so that the dirt had no place to hide. This was the only time of high anxiety and fear that I ever experienced in school and my nail picking habit that curses me to this day started then.

During the long winter, I loved spending the evenings in my grandmother's kitchen watching the sewing, washing of wool and knitting. The sewing machine was the pedal kind and I was fascinated by it. Old sweaters were unravelled and the wool was washed, dried and rewound. I remember my arms getting very tired holding skeins of wool while my grandmother or my sister wound the balls.

Being quite small, I was eventually excused and allowed into my grandmother's parlor. There I practiced my braiding on the fringes of her curtains or played with the cylindrical bolsters that provided backrests on her 2 narrow beds. The rug had a wonderful flower design with square sections that made perfect roads and I spent hours playing with matchbox cars around and under her dining room table.

Chapter 4 - 1963

With my aunt's help, we were the second ones in our building to get a black and white television. It sat in 'our' living room, close to the door. Our father would turn it towards the door and we sat on the kitchen floor to watch it, as we weren't allowed into 'his' room. It had a small screen the size of a handkerchief and no remote, as they hadn't been invented yet. Being older, the first time my sister remembers seeing a TV was in a neighbour's apartment downstairs. The two children's shows I remember us watching were: 'The Mickey Mouse Club' and 'Zorro' with Guy Williams. I also remember watching, '*Dobranoc*' -Goodnight, which came on at 8 p.m. for maybe 10-15 minutes. It used ping pong balls as the heads for two hand puppets. We would try to copy them by making our own puppets, anytime we found an old ping pong ball.

Basia and I were dressed alike and put to bed at the same time. Though we were very different, we were treated as if we were twins. Children are born with a strong sense of fairness and I imagine that being three and a half years older, that did not seem fair to her and increased her resentment. I think that because of this, having to share a room proved very difficult and prevented us from growing closer as we grew older.

In contrast, I staggered my children's bedtimes by age and made sure they had their own rooms and respected each other's privacy.

Once again on my birthday, my mother showed the love that she was able to show, by waking me up with a waffle/chocolate tort and candles. Homemade torts used several large (12 inch) thin layers of waffle with a chocolate paste in between.

You might know these specialty waffles as Prince Polo which have been made in my hometown of Cieszyn in one form or another, since 1921. After the war the factory was nationalized and named Olza. Our neighbour worked there. When we asked why she didn't bring any chocolate home, we were told that she could eat as much as she liked at work but could not take any home. How lucky for her, but she was also the only person that we knew who developed diabetes. No wonder as she was one of only two people that was overweight.

By the age of eight or nine, we knew every street within a two kilometre radius like the back of our hands. For no reason at all except to indulge our joy of exploration, we would run down to the old castle ruins and up the ladders to the top of the still standing tower. We'd visit the well that our town was famous for. We'd check out the long lines of people waiting to cross to Czechoslovakia at the border bridge. Or we'd visit the library, the farmer's market or the stationary store. We'd go to the Catholic cemetery and water flowers there, just for something to do. And played on our favourite statue of Mieszko in our little forest park.

I remember one day my friend Małgosia from downstairs, suggested that I come along with her on an errand to deliver something to her aunt in a neighbouring village. I had never been on a bus. How impressed I was that she being eight, a year younger than I, knew how to travel by herself. Without telling anyone in my family we walked down to the bus station and found the bus to take us to Dzięgielów, about a 20 minute journey each way. We spent maybe an hour there having tea and looking around then took the bus home. It's like it was a totally normal thing to do.

Having finished grade 2 as the top student for the second year in a row, I once again received a book as my prize. My father just shrugged his shoulders, told me it was no less than he expected and returned his attention to his newspaper.

My family of choice

And so my path was set and the search was on. For if your own father considers you unlovable, then there is nothing to lose. And courage is easier if you have nothing to lose. And that's great, because there is then a replacement to be sought.

My father worked as an accountant for Celma, a company that made electric tools. When I turned nine, Basia and I were sent to the company summer camp on the Baltic Sea. I was the youngest in our cabin and we had a young teacher as our den mother. This was the only way she and her new husband were able to afford a honeymoon at the seaside with her husband coming along on our excursions. Being the youngest and smallest, I always seemed to lag behind and he, bringing up the rear, would hoist me up on his shoulders. Before long, I had my first feelings of belonging. I felt truly cherished by this couple. They told me that I was the child that they dreamed of, and could they pretend that I was their daughter until they had their own? I was thrilled to encounter someone else who shared my fantasy even for a summer month. Destiny was looking out for me because they came from the same town as I and that meant that we could continue the relationship after camp was over.

It turned out that they lived a few blocks from our apartment and Janusz's professor father was friends with my grandmother. I frequently visited them and would introduce them to my friends as my 'heart' parents. I had finally found the harmony, laughter and love that I had been seeking.

My new father Janusz was an engineer at the nearby coal mines. He was a great engineer as he had a disciplined mind that was characterized by high accuracy and precision in everything he did. His wife Irena was an elementary school teacher and truly the most beautiful woman in town. She was so beautiful that she had offers to become an actress. But she was very happy being a wife and mother. They had a collie dog named Ramuś, a fish tank, a canary, a hamster or guinea pig and a turtle. Since I had a standing invitation to visit, I would pick dandelion leaves and go over to feed the turtle and play with their beautiful dog, occasionally bringing a friend. They told me how much they were looking forward to having children of their own, but for now, we pretended that I was theirs. I had manifested a new set of parents; secret parents who loved me how I envisioned real parents would love their child.

Belonging to a loving family meant everything to me. It was a need that resonated from deep within, and just because I wasn't born into one, I had just been successful in creating it, and that made me feel jubilant.

Little did I know that the strong urge came from many past lives of close family life, and it was not what Destiny had in store for balancing my spiritual development in this one…

I went into grade 3. The teacher was the same Pani Marosz. I remember that one evening after dark, she organized our class to meet her by the school so that she could explain the stars to us. This made a great impression on me.

'Recycling'

Each year I became more conscious of my environment and how it functioned. Everything was either repaired or recycled. We returned soda bottles and beer bottles to the store. The store sent them back to the plant to be washed and sterilized and refilled, so it could use the same bottles over and over. There was no such thing as plastic or styrofoam containers to throw away.

Kids got hand-me-down clothes from their brothers or sisters, or their mothers sewed them. And if a button fell off, a seam unravelled or a sock got a hole in it, we knew how to fix it. Shoes, belts, purses and bags went to the shoemaker for repairs. As children, we were taught how to clean, polish and shine leather shoes: our own as well as our parents'.

In the kitchen, everything was blended and stirred by hand. No one had any kind of electric gadget, not even a vacuum cleaner. Floors were swept and area rugs were hung outside on a wooden carpet railing called a *'trzepak'* (from the word *trzepać*, "to beat"). Children also used it as a soccer goal and for gymnastics. The wicker beater itself was called a *'trzepaczka'*.

Outside, lawns were cut with a sickle or a scythe and occasionally with a push mower, like at the rectory house beside us.

Back then, people didn't fire up an engine and burn gasoline - they got their exercise through walking and housework, so there was no need for sport clubs or gyms.

Some were lucky enough to own a washing machine, otherwise all washing was done with a tub and a washboard. I remember having to help wring out sheets by holding each end and twisting them. Laundry was then hung and dried on a clothesline outside - wind and solar power really did the job and the sun bleached and sterilized them. Including menstrual pads and baby's diapers.

The one thing that now might be considered a luxury was that large items such as bed linens, towels, curtains and tablecloths - those items which would be cumbersome and ineffective to iron at home, were sent to '*magiel*' - a place that had machines for ironing with the use of a roller system. After washing at home, these larger items of linen were starched, ironed and folded there for a nominal price. Starch was very popular. There were no synthetics like polyester, so everything wrinkled. We had a washing machine that had to be filled with water from the tap in the hallway and there was another tap on the machine to empty it. It had to be filled and emptied several times. Since there was no easy way to produce hot water, many items had to be pre-soaked.

When a fragile item needed to be packaged for mailing, a wadded up old newspaper was used to cushion it, not styrofoam or plastic bubble wrap.

The most common pens were dipped in a bottle of ink. The more pricey ones had a cartridge that was refilled from an ink bottle instead of buying a new pen. In both cases we had to use a blotter so the ink wouldn't smudge before it dried. I remember the first time one of my classmates brought in a '*długopis*' - a ballpoint pen. We were all enthralled. No mess!

Men replaced the razor blades in a razor instead of throwing away the whole razor just because the blade got dull.

There were three small metal trash bins for the 18 apartments in our building and the few items that went into them were truly unrecyclable.

Work

In grade 8, at the age of 13-14, children were tested as to ability and prepared for entry into several different secondary schools. There was an academic highschool, a technical highschool, culinary and agricultural one. There were also shorter training programs for store clerks, factory workers and construction labor.

There were no homeless people or drug addicts. No vagrants lay on the sidewalks or in parks and no child was without a safe bed to sleep in. Doors did not need to be locked as there was nothing to steal. Everyone had a job and a roof over their head. No matter how basic and boring the food might have been, no one went hungry. Very few people were overweight or had diabetes, and allergies were unheard of.

And no one complained because we were all in the same boat. Family and neighbours looked out for each other: young as well as elderly members were tended to without any compensation. It was simply considered to be the humane thing to do.

People walked to the grocery store and to work. If the distance was too great, there was a streetcar or a bus in the bigger towns and cities. Starting in grade one, children walked to and from school. Unattended. And we certainly didn't climb into a 120 horsepower machine every time we had to go three blocks. Quite a contrast to today's society where moms are turned into a 24-hour taxi service. Most regular people managed to save enough money to buy a car only by the time they retired.

We used cotton net bags for carrying groceries and aluminum 'banki' for purchasing milk. Some items were wrapped in brown paper and tied with string. The paper and string were reused in the home many times over. In the stores, all the items (and there weren't many) were behind the counter and a customer had to request the items they wanted. There was no such thing as picking up, inspecting and choosing things yourself. The downside of this was that there was no incentive to excel and no risk of being fired, so cashiers and clerks were sometimes too busy to serve customers because they were 'doing their nails'. One had to be extremely polite when speaking to them or they wouldn't help you at all.

Each adult had to be self supporting even if it meant having a job that was far from fulfilling. If a person had absolutely no skills, they contributed by working in the fields, sweeping sidewalks or emptying the public metal trash baskets that stood on every corner. Everyone was taught to be useful. It was everyone's responsibility to speak up and correct children so that they wouldn't turn into hooligans as society though poor, strived to become more and more civilized.

Christmas

I remember the time leading up to Christmas. December 4th was St. Barbara's Day and as it was my sister's name day, she received a gift or two. This was a Catholic tradition and again, I'm surprised that my father went along with celebrating it.

I took every opportunity to open the closets and cupboards in my grandmother's living/bedroom. This is the only time that I remember being very excited about Christmas and I think this is the year I got the big bear. Then several days before Christmas, the door was locked.

My father secured the traditional live carp for our Christmas dinner. A week or two before, I'd find them swimming in the bathtub. On the afternoon of Christmas Eve, while my sister and I were finally being bathed again, the now breaded carp filets and under my father's watchful eye, were jumping on the frying pan. The rest of the fish including the eyes was turned into delicious soup.

Christmas Eve dinner is still clear to me, though there are no pictures. It was one of the few rare days that my father allowed his mother to have her way. When the first star appeared in the sky, we all sat down at a long table in my grandmother's kitchen. Beside each place setting was a little candle and an *Opłatek* which is a wafer made of flour and water embossed with a religious image. We then shared pieces of it with everyone else along with good wishes for health and prosperity.

Although this meal was reserved for the closest family, it was customary to set an extra place for an unexpected guest or even a vagrant. No one was to be turned away if they knocked on the door on this holy night.

Most of the dishes were cooked only once a year, specifically for Christmas. We had the traditional borscht broth with small pierogies. There was pickled herring. We had the fish, along with potato salad made with eggs and pickles. For dessert there was poppy seed roll and babka, gingerbread cake and a wide assortment of homemade cookies. My grandmother's anise and angel wing cookies were my favorite. There was even chocolate that was prepared before Christmas as it required being cooled quickly. Since fridges were extremely difficult to obtain in Poland, the cookie sheets were set out on the snow outside.

The greatest novelty of all was when we got an orange each for the first time.

After dinner, my grandmother read the story from her Bible after which she started singing her favorite Christmas Carol called '*Lulajże Jezuniu*'. We then sang some more Christmas songs while my father excused himself. Then he opened the door and we were led into my grandmother's living area where we saw the Christmas tree for the first time. It was decorated and lit with small candles. There were some presents underneath. I can still easily recall the sight of it. I only have this one memory so I don't know if there was only one Christmas, or if they were all the same.

On New Year's Eve my mother made pączki - boiled jam filled donuts in oil. There was usually a dress up party around this time. There was no such thing as Halloween.

Chapter 5 - 1964

Spring came and with it a molded sheep treat made from marzipan and sugar given to children each Easter. And the braided egg bread called '*chałka*'. There were also compulsory volunteer work days which intentionally fell on religious days. These were organized by the government for community services such as cleaning streets, fixing public amenities and collecting recyclable materials. Then came the compulsory May 1st parade.

Around this time my father gave me a book to read by American born James Oliver Curwood who in 1927 was the highest paid author in the world. He wrote action adventure stories based in the Hudson Bay, Yukon and Alaska areas. The book my father gave me was the Polish translation of "The Wolf Hunters" followed by the sequel "The Gold Hunters". I suspect this author was also my aunt Lidia's favourite as during WW2, she escaped and embarked on a life of a pioneer in the Canadian wilderness and later named her dog after his book "Kazan".

I remember this being my first 'grown up' book. Looking back I wonder if my father was trying to acquaint me with Canada?

I turned ten years old and was allowed to organize my own birthday party in our apartment without my parents around. Danusia and I decided who I should invite. She was sweet on Janusz and because all the girls liked him, he was the only boy that got invited. I really wanted to invite Waldek, who I had a crush on since we danced together in kindergarten, but I was just too shy.

I continued to do really well in school and for the third year in a row, I received the top marks in my class and the coveted reward of a book. I was sure that my parents would finally love me the way that I saw my friends and cousins being loved, cherished, encouraged and rewarded. I was the top student three years in a row but sadly, upon sharing my good news, all I got was "you're looking for approval? We expect no less than perfection from you." But having so many other loving people in my life, my parents' opinion didn't really matter that much.

On TV we were now able to watch 'The Saint' with Roger Moore. All the shows from other countries were dubbed into Polish by a man speaking all the character parts.

On August 17, my chosen parents welcomed a baby boy. They named him Krzysio. They called me 'big sister' and assured me that I would always be 'their child' as well. I was thrilled that they still continued to think of me as their 'daughter'.

In the fall I started grade 4 with Pan Żyla who excelled in music. This was the sixth year that our kindergarten group had been together. One of the few things I remember was how he rearranged the classroom so that the worst student sat with the best one and so on. I remember that Krzysztof Sitek shared my desk. One day one of the two worst behaved boys Andrzej Gruszka threw a stale bun through the window and it hit Pan Żyla on the head. He ran out and chased him down. Andrzej Polok was another one. and Liwocha. He disciplined them by knocking their heads together.

Our class was the most troublesome but also the most intelligent. And above all, we bonded for life.

That July Basia and I went to Gdańsk with our Babusia. Babusia and I sent my mother a postcard from a famous cathedral. There,we also met up with a Czech auntie and her daughter. Someone took a picture of us in front of a big ship called 'Batory'.

Transition

My life was overall very happy. Ninety percent of it revolved around friends, community and school where for the most part, children were kept together from kindergarten to eighth grade. I loved that.

The communist system raised me for the second five years of my life and frankly, I think my parents were relieved not to have the burden. I didn't mind - as my parents were a negligible part of it and as long as I stayed silent and out of their way, they tolerated me. In their view, a voice was a privilege acquired with growing up, along with loose hair, nail polish, makeup and heels. Their role was quite minor in my life. Their negativity and lack of love was easily overridden by my sense of belonging to the state and having a place in many other people's hearts. I excelled in school, I was nurtured by the neighbors and most important of all, 'adopted' by a wonderful couple and to make my life complete, I was now a big 'sister'.

The indoctrination of idealistic character traits by the communist school system gave me a wonderful childhood. I was a valuable part of the future and we were learning obedience and responsibility. And I was very, very good at that. I was well indoctrinated that if I was a good, loyal and honest citizen, the system would look after me.

Except for the stark contrast of family attitudes, I loved my childhood and everything else about it. Almost unlimited freedom and safety to explore, such as is unheard of for children under eleven in today's society. This of course came along with clear rules and expectations. I didn't mind the poverty of communism at all. I loved the stability of living at the same, though cramped address. I loved my school, my neighborhood and my beautiful, historic town.

We must be willing to let go of the life we have planned, so as to have the life that is waiting for us - E.M. Forster

My lovely world came to an end in late October. It was unusual for my mother to ask Małgosia's seamstress mom to sew pants and a jacket for me as she was a competent seamstress and made many of our clothes. My favourite item that she sewed for me, was a skirt made from a circle. How I loved twirling around in that!

I don't remember being told that we were leaving. All of a sudden there was a lot of activity. I was told that I could pick out two of my favorite toys. I was in shock that my life as I knew it was coming to an end without any warning. I did not know what was going on, but there was a lot of packing, so I took my favorite toy, my big bear, downstairs to Małgosia's place for safekeeping. I remember stealing away to see my heart family and divulged the secret to them while thinking that they now had a replacement for me and likely my time as their daughter was finished. But I wrote down their address anyway.

My sister thinks that she was told two weeks in advance and sworn to secrecy. If the word got out someone would likely have reported us and we would have been prevented from leaving. Basia also remembers the growing pile of stuff in our grandmother's apartment as our parents quickly emptied ours.

My anxiety level rose so much that I got ill with a fever. I could not bear the thought of leaving. Questions were not allowed and no explanations were given. I caused a great deal of concern, as my parents needed to have a health certificate for us all. Finally someone bribed a nurse to sign one without seeing me. The next morning we were hurried out to a waiting automobile and drove off. I had no chance to retrieve my bear. All I had was an expensive new doll I had recently received, that meant nothing to me.

I don't remember much of the drive. I imagine I slept most of the way. I assume that we then took the train and arrived at the port in Gdynia where my parents, my grandmother, my sister and I boarded the refurbished military transport ship M.S. Batory that had been built in 1936.

Years later I wondered whatever would have possessed my grandmother, age 65, to leave her world behind, even for the one year visit to see her daughter. She was very much a woman of the old country and was highly respected there. I found out years later from my father's cousins Marysia and her twin sister Irka, that my grandmother was asked by her boss for her hand in marriage. But this was the 1960's and her children were unable to see her in any other role but as their mother and they were vehemently opposed to such an idea. When she returned a year later, Pan W. Krupa, assuming she had gone for good, had already married another. And so my grandmother shut down her life there and returned to Toronto heartbroken.

The ocean voyage took eleven days and being the end of October, the Atlantic was stormy. The second day I got quite seasick and remained so for the rest of the trip. I must have slept again. All I remember is being on the top wooden bunk in a small crowded cabin without windows that we shared with another family.

On November 9, 1964 my dad's sister met us in Montreal. She and her friend Stanley brought two cars. As the ship allowed unlimited baggage, my father had packed their bedding and his books but I could not bring any of my well loved books, favorite blanket or pillow. We spent the night with Lidia's friend in Montreal and ate Rice Krispies for breakfast.

My aunt lived in a new duplex in the Don Mills suburb of Toronto at 40 Pinemore Crescent. The four of us were given the master bedroom to live in for the next 8-9 months. My grandmother got one of the smaller bedrooms, while Lidia moved to the 3rd. Jurek was moved into the basement.

Shortly after our arrival, Aunt Lidia took us to Eaton's and bought us thick, wool, beige car coats with pegs instead of buttons and hoods.

I now had to start life as a 'baby' again. No language, no mobility, and a completely different set of rules. Not only that, the people that I felt the least connection to, were now 90% of my support base. To me it felt like being kidnapped whereas for my sister at almost 14 years of age, it was an adventure. And my parents turned into these bitter 'strangers' who were faced with their own struggles to adjust, and were even more irritable, rejecting and critical. I focused on staying out of their way, rarely being seen or heard.

In my mother's defence, she never wanted to leave her beloved Warsaw for the small town where her husband's family lived, never mind leaving the old country to go somewhere that was as different as another planet.

I found out years later that when my father suggested getting out and moving to Canada, she was completely opposed. He then made a deal with her: if she cooperated with the application, he would move us to Warsaw where we would live until such time that we were given permission to emigrate. This was 1964 and no one was being allowed to leave, never mind whole families. So she was confident that it would never happen while living back in Warsaw would be a dream come true for her. And thus she agreed to the deal.

And this is where Destiny interfered. Somehow, somewhere, someone in charge was asleep at their desk, and against all odds, our papers were approved and passports were issued. This was unheard of in 1964.

So she had no more say: in her mind, God had spoken. She now had to be the dutiful wife under her husband's authoritarian rule. Her main function was to 'keep the peace' at all cost and model martyrdom for her daughters.

Once again, she reminded us never to accept compliments as it would bring some disaster on us, or at least bad luck. Always deny it or invalidate it. She would also remind me not to do anything to bring attention to myself because people would get jealous and have ill will toward us. Funny, the only person I ever felt ill-will from, was my mother. And resentment from her was strong anytime something good happened to me during the rest of my life. It was as if she was envious that since she didn't get good things, she didn't wish them for me. If she had to be a martyr, then so did I.

I no longer had anyone else to contradict this influence. And in a country that lauded self promotion and extroverts, this advice would prove to be severely damaging in every aspect of my life.

Re-education

Several days later I was taken to my new school. Having been in grade 4 in Poland, I was put into a grade 4 class where I was a year older than everyone else because kids in Canada started school at age six. My sister, who was in grade 8, was placed in grade 7 of middle school, in order to have a chance to learn English before entering highschool.

I was the only child, not only in the classroom, but also in the school that did not know a single word of English. What a wonderful surprise that each morning started with the anthem and the Lord's Prayer. There were no accommodations for immigrants in the suburbs: no 'New Canadian' classes for teaching English language and customs, but those two things helped me to feel the country unity that I was joining. And my teacher Mrs. McPhearson was great. She started by drawing pictures and labeling them. I was then instructed to copy the words and learn to spell them. My new classmates made fun of my attempts at pronouncing English words, but within six months I was excelling in spelling bees without even knowing many of the words.

Math was easy; Poland taught that curriculum in grade 2 and my grade 4 math skills carried me through well into grade 7.

My aunt had recruited the kids next door to walk me to school. There were five children in the Lucas family, three boys and two girls. The older girl's name was Kristin and she was a year younger than I. Her oldest brother's name was Eric and they were friendly and included me when they played outside. They had wonderful toys. They got a good laugh when I tried to teach them some of my childhood games using sticks, chalk and pebbles.

Across the street lived a girl that was in my class and she took over walking me to school. Her name was Nancy.

In the evenings TV was my escape and there was now no limit as to how much I could watch. My favorite show was "The Man From U.N.C.L.E." I credit Illya Kuryakin with teaching me as much english as I learned at school! I also made attempts to copy his accent and for many years, people who met me thought I was from Britain.

I remember Jurek and I standing at the kitchen counter and discussing my name. I insisted that I should be called Isia and not Irene. He insisted that Isia was too difficult for Canadians to pronounce and came up with Rini by taking the i from the front of Irene and making the two 'e' letters from 'rene' into 'i's. It was decided: I had a new name that stayed with me through highschool though I never felt that I was really me until I changed back to Isha.

He mentioned a letter that he had written in reply to mine. I asked my parents about it and they produced the letter dated October 8, 1964, that they withheld from me as it mentioned the plan to leave and they were afraid that I was too young to keep the secret.

"Dearest Isia.

Thank you very much for your beautiful letter, which I received a few days ago, along with a postcard from Basia.

Most of all I liked the description of the cathedral because I am studying architecture and will continue this direction at university. I am happy that you are enjoying your vacation. This year I am not spending my vacation at Scout camp like in the past, instead I looked for work for the first week and then went up north with a friend for a week.

As soon as I got back, I found out that I was accepted at an office. I am working there for the rest of the summer and am earning $150 per month. I wanted to buy myself a motorcycle but I give most of it to my mom and will buy school books with the rest.

Kazan lost weight over the summer because he's running around more, but otherwise is fantastic.

I am very happy that you all will come, but I'm concerned that it will be a bit crowded as we only have three bedrooms and a living room.

Kisses and see you in Canada - Jurek"

I remember getting a pair of used skates for Christmas and my 17 year old cousin Jurek's attempts to teach me to skate, though I never improved, as I just couldn't master the stopping part. But he was kind - though as a teenager I'm sure he wasn't thrilled to be invaded by five relatives from the old country. Fortunately he was fluent in Polish.

Lifeline

Amazingly my heart family never broke the bond. My heart dad Janusz wrote letters to me regularly even though I was not consistent with my replies. At Christmas he enclosed an '*opłatek*'.

I visited them in my dreams, which became my reality. So it didn't really matter that I didn't write back. There was no money for stamps and my parents strongly discouraged me from keeping in touch with anyone back home.

Though my life was bearable, I still hadn't gotten over the shock. I was severely homesick. I coped by pretending that the waking time was really the dream and that when I fell asleep, I was back in my real life. Hence most nights, I begged to go to bed as early as I could, which was usually around 7:30pm. Then I was back home at school with my friends, playing near my home, and walking the cobblestone streets. This lasted for two years.

I can't imagine what it must have been like for my grandmother: new language, new customs, no friends and no 'village' to walk around and shop where she was known. She had lived in that world for 65 years and gave it up for her daughter. At first she came for a visit and I'm sure Lidia was on her best behavior and would have 'lost face' if she couldn't be the hero, rescuing her mother from Communism. If my grandmother had gone back, I would have begged to go back as well. I wonder how my cousin Jurek remembers it…

What touched my heart most was that my 'heart' father wrote that he and his wife often talked to their children about their 'big sister' in Canada. Twelve years later when I finally was able to go back for a visit, I got tears in my eyes when, being introduced to their friends, neighbors and relatives, I was greeted with "Ah, you're the Canadian daughter we've heard so much about." It confirmed to me that I hadn't just imagined the strength of bond I felt, simply because I needed to feel it: it was mutual and it was my lifeline. There was absolutely nothing in it for him to be writing to me over those many years. It remains lodged in my mind as a moment of immense kindness.

Several of my classmates wrote to me as well, begging me to send them ballpoint pens. Ola Knobloch was the most consistent even though we weren't close friends at the time. Even Waldek wrote to me professing the love he couldn't express when I lived there. Each letter and postcard that I received, gave me a combination of great joy and sadness. Emotions that were very difficult for a ten year old to process. This experience taught me that with a little bit of effort, true long term relationships could be sustained in spite of overwhelming obstacles.

Contrast

The world that my parents and grandparents lived in was very similar to the first ten years of my life. Apart from fashion, there had been little progress in Eastern Europe since the turn of the century. And WW2 had set society back to basics. We lived in the same dwellings, ate the same food, used the same items, did the same chores and read many of the same books as the previous two generations. How different everything was when it came time to raise my children in another country!

Coming from a town that had existed for over a thousand years, to a western country that was less than 100 years old, was a huge contrast. I found Canada to be too boisterous, too wild and too uncivilized.

Whenever the topic came up with other immigrants, it turned out that the pre-teens had the greatest difficulty adjusting. Apart from the trauma of moving to a different country halfway across the world, others that I have spoken to agree that age nine to eleven is the worst time to 'transplant' a child.

Ch 6 - 1965

Shortly after the New Year, school brought its own trauma and consequences. While walking in the school yard, I was hit across the mouth by a hockey stick being swung by a classmate coming around the corner of the building.

This serious accident knocked my four top teeth so loose and I was sent home. My parents had no choice but to be concerned and after rebuking me for my carelessness that caused trouble for them, took me to the cheapest dentist they could find. He in his incompetence increased the damage by drilling through these teeth and inserting posts inside. It was an awful nightmare for me, much worse than the accident. And due to this procedure, the dental damage would become tragic just three years later.

Because of such poor judgement I now struggled with trusting the authority of my parents even more. We were still living with Aunt Lidia. My Babusia seemed even more powerless than I, and my aunt was rarely home. And when she was, she often isolated herself due to severe migraines.

I had no one else to turn to and therefore did not tell anyone about something else that was wrong. It was the discomfort I felt when children teased me about something being wrong with my eye. It turned out that I had a 'lazy eye': my left eye did not move sideways like it should have, as the muscles holding the eyeball were too tight. Why hadn't my parents taken care of it in Poland? This could have been easily fixed before age six, with an eyepatch or even a simple surgery. Perhaps they were just too busy to notice.

Now I was saddled with another thing to be self conscious about and in order to avoid comments, I stopped looking at people. At the tender age of ten and a half, I felt severely wounded, helpless and alone. I learned to be invisible so as not to be scolded. My lack of the English language intensified my hesitancy to speak up. This locked me into a world of waking silence and increased my determination to escape into my comforting dreams.

The worst tragedy in life is not being wanted or loved as a child because the belief sets in at a very young age that 'if my own mother (or parents) doesn't find me worth loving, then how can anyone else?'

It was 1965 and I lived at the tail end of the generation when it was still very respectable and much valued to be a stay at home mother. Though it wasn't modelled in my family, I saw the contrast: I was given the strong impression that it was a noble goal to pursue, and a very desirable lifestyle for children. In Canada a good man took great pride from being able to provide for his family so that their most important asset, their young children, were well loved and infused full time with their family values. In Canada, parents were allowed to show that they valued their children. In Communist Poland, the state's goal was to separate children from their mothers at a very young age under the guise of 'valuing' them both. The Communist system strongly discouraged family loyalty but there was no doubt that it valued children. That way they were able to indoctrinate the next generation to be loyal to the state, right from the most impressionable years.

I now saw how fortunate I was to have had my mother stay home during my preschool years and how that was the only time that I actually felt like I was valuable enough for her to do that. Now I only felt like a burden and a bother. I filed that in my memory for the future.

In order to help them function in their new country, my parents were required to attend 'New Canadian' language classes but the priority was on finding work as soon as possible. My aunt who sponsored us had to work because she was a single mother, but my new friends' mothers did not.

My mother was able to get a job first, at the Timex wrist watch factory. She had better 'luck' because of her superior diligence and cooperative attitude. My aunt eventually got my father a job as a stock boy at Eaton's department store where they gave him the nickname Jack as they couldn't pronounce Zbigniew. I remember he was very unhappy there. This was not his dream of life in Canada, the country flowing with milk and honey that his sister promised him. Whereas my mother did what was required without complaint.

After seven months of school in a new language, I finished grade 4 with marks that were in line with an average Canadian born 10 year old child. No special classes or consideration whatsoever. Though getting top marks was now difficult, by the end of the school year I had enough of a grasp to be able to pass grade 4 with a C average. It took me another year to regain the 'top of the class' status. My father was still not impressed and all I got was "you're looking for approval? We expect no less than perfection from you." I was young, naive, isolated and desperate.

My escape into sleep and 'astral' travel home, continued for another year.

Though I had just turned eleven, in my waking hours, I did my best to advance from the toddler that I'd become not being able to speak or get around, to a functioning pre-teen.

There was a Becker's convenience store in the plaza nearby (Parkway Mall) and I remember being sent to buy milk in a glass gallon jug. My aunt told me that milk used to be delivered to homes and that's why there was a square nook called a milk box in the wall by the back door. It had a small door on the inside and outside of the home. I also remember begging for 10 cents to ride the mechanical horse at that plaza. I was much too big, but to me, it was a marvelous invention. It took some convincing over several weeks but eventually I was given the dime.

When summer came, my aunt organized a trip for the seven of us to Niagara Falls.

Then I was sent to Polish Scout camp near Barry's Bay for a month. Meanwhile my parents packed us up and moved us into a 2 bedroom walkup downtown, at 801 Shaw Street. It was close to Christie Pits Park where Basia and I sometimes went swimming in the public pool or to play on the swings. But the unexpected adjustment was difficult once again: new neighbourhood, new school. I felt ripped away once more just as I was beginning to adjust. And somehow, my precious terrier broach went missing. Another loss.

This was the first of a series of eight moves that were very difficult for me and added to my inability to make the kind of friendships that I left behind and so desperately needed. It also damaged my trust in my unsentimental parents, as they made the decisions as to which of my meager possessions were no longer useful and were therefore discarded. Each year arriving back from camp I'd realise that many of my treasures were gone.

Then I stopped speaking

These conditions led to my childhood development of selective mutism which was a self protection mechanism.

"Besides lack of speech, other common behaviors and characteristics displayed by selectively mute people include:

- *Difficulty maintaining eye contact*
- *Blank expression and reluctance to smile*
- *Stiff and awkward movements*

- *Difficulty expressing feelings, even to family members*
- *Excessive shyness, fear of social embarrassment, and/or social isolation and withdrawal*
- *Tendency to worry more than most people of the same age*
- *Desire for routine and dislike of changes*
- *Sensitivity to noise and crowds*
- *Moodiness*
- *Sleep problems*

On the positive side, many sufferers have:
- *Above-average intelligence, perception, or inquisitiveness*
- *Creativity and a love for art or music*
- *Empathy and sensitivity to others' thoughts and feelings*
- *A strong sense of right and wrong"*

I still struggle with some remnants of this disorder which plagued me as an immigrant child of an oppressive father.

My circle of support shrank even more

The four of us now lived on the second floor

and sometimes my father and sister would climb out the kitchen window onto the back porch roof and up a ladder onto the roof of the third story, but I was told that I was too young. They would go up to adjust our TV antenna or just look at the view. I waited for them on that back porch roof.

In September, I started grade 5 at Essex Public School, in Mr. Davidson's class. Like in Poland, I wore my hair in two braids pretty much every day. I suspect because of that, my strong accent, and my hesitation to speak, it wasn't long before I became a target for beatings by a school bully. He would lie in wait for me then push me and punch me. This occurred on an almost daily basis along my fifteen minute route to school. I had never encountered this kind of behavior in my life! My parents blamed me and told me that it must be something that I was doing wrong. My father told me that either I must have done something to provoke it, or that "life was an eat or be eaten situation" and it would make me stronger. The pattern never changed: the other person was always defended. No one did anything wrong, it was always my fault. My mother would observe this and I had a feeling that she was gloating. It was inconceivable to me how a mother could show such a feeling of almost happy triumph at her daughter's misfortune. It wasn't until many years later that I found out how much my father berated her and I suppose this made her feel less targeted. The result was that they both refused to intervene and my aunt was too far away to help.

Once again it was up to me to figure things out for myself, but this time I was in a strange country. Though by this time I spoke less and studied more, I had to do something. I noticed a girl in my class that walked in the same direction so I started following her after school to her home and then ran the rest of the way to mine. Soon I was almost her shadow. Carolyn Drewer was kind and after a week or so, she would wait for me close to where I lived so that we would walk to school together.

Basia and I were allowed to get a small pet and we chose a small green turtle. We kept it in a round tank often setting it on the window sill. One day the turtle was gone. I don't know if a bird took it or what, but because it was my fault, I was deemed too irresponsible for another.

In December, the four of us had Christmas dinner on the coffee table in the living room. I remember a lot of snow so that is perhaps the reason we did not celebrate with Aunt Lidia. My 'heart' father Janusz again sent me an '*Opłatek*'.

Chapter 7 - 1966

Every recess we were sent outside, rain or shine. In the winter there was a long icy slide in the school yard. The fun was short lived for me as I fell and cracked a bone in my left forearm. My parents didn't hesitate to remind me what a bother I was. I remember having a long bandage wrapped around a steel support that was attached from my elbow to the palm of my hand.

Sometime in the spring, my father bought his first car, a 'Prinz' made by NSU Motorworks, a motorcycle manufacturer, in Germany. This model was made from 1958-1962. It was a tiny car, so light that once or twice while it was parallel parked on the street, four youths picked it up and set it down sideways, perpendicular to the sidewalk. My mother then learned to drive and used it to get to work.

I was a very conscientious student and at the end of the school year received top marks in my class. The only student promoted from grade 5 to grade 7, I skipped grade 6 altogether. My teacher thought it would also be beneficial for me to enter grade seven with my age group of twelve year olds. I remember feeling penalized for working so hard, as this would mean a totally new group of classmates in the fall. Once again there was no acknowledgement or approval at home.

The landlord had a bicycle and allowed us to use it. I rejoiced at this new found freedom. It was a ladies bike, no hand brakes and much too big for me. I could only touch the pedals when I was off the seat and the breaking was done with the pedals. What stands out for me is the memory of gliding down a lane in joyous abandon when I realized that I was coming close to an intersection. I was unable to step on the pedals and stop. I rode across the road to the sound of screeching car brakes. I think that's the closest I ever came to death.

I never told my parents as I knew they would just make me feel worse. But I never rode that bike again.

There was no 'gang' for me to hang out with and no errands to run. At the age of 12, I felt deeply the lack of purpose and more useless than I had at 7. And I loved feeling useful: it gave my life meaning. Now there were no friends or neighbors to provide a sense of belonging. On our occasional weekend visits to aunt Lidia's house, Basia and I contributed by cutting the grass in the front and back with a push mower. I think Jurek had a job and a girlfriend so it fell to us in order to spare our 67 year old Babusia from the task. There were other attempts at this age to make myself useful but it was very different from the life of a child in Poland. I remember using Ajax powder to clean the side of my aunt's fridge but that didn't turn out well as it took the shine right off along with any dirt.

One time Lidia's ex-husband arrived for a visit and he told Basia that he would pay her if she painted Lidia's fence. Our father put a stop to that when he found out.

Love requires certain actions to be voluntary

I remember a time when my father was in the mood to socialize, and we joined some newly arrived relatives for a day at Center Island. We took the ferry and I remember begging to go on a pony ride there. That's all it took for me to fall in love with horseback riding. How nice my father could be to me when others were around. My father had the ability to present himself well: caring, funny, warm and friendly. I understand how people could see him in such a positive light because they knew him only at a superficial level. Those who were closest to him such as his mother, his sister, his wife and his two daughters knew all too well what really lurked behind this facade: a diehard misogynist. There was no affection whatsoever: never as much as a hug or a word of encouragement or approval. Yet he constantly reminded us that he was doing everything for us.

Now that we were living away from my aunt's and my grandmother's protection, the emotional abuse intensified. Sharing any happy event with my father such as an invitation to Carolyn's birthday party, led to lectures on his favorite topic of indoctrination. I remember those words clearly as they were repeated often throughout my childhood: "People don't really want you around. If they invite you, they are just being polite, they don't really mean it. So don't embarrass yourself by accepting."

I had never heard this in Poland, but there, he was a very small part of my life. Now, instead of being able to continue to experience my childhood assuming that I was welcome to join other children and not having anyone to contradict his words, I started to believe him. Along with my hesitant speech and the trials of puberty, I turned more and more awkward. I became repressed, apologetic and exceedingly well behaved due to my new belief that I could no longer simply assume that I was welcome anywhere, and should never impose myself on anyone. I followed my sister's example and became a voracious reader in order to cope.

More and more, I saw a new side of my father for the first time. He was not only emotionally and verbally abusive, he had a mean streak. He was an unhappy man whose dream life after two years in Canada was now a crushing disappointment beyond his control, and he couldn't allow anyone under his control to be happy. I remember getting in trouble for laughing or expressing joy. A bit of this programming cripples me from within to this day.

Perhaps because he felt no control over his life, he started to make more and more rules for us. It was a huge change for me to have no activities outside the home and I felt like I was not only living in a foreign country that I felt no connection to, I was becoming very aware that I was living a life without purpose or love.

By the age of 12, I had lost the richness of my life as well as my awareness of, and the connection to my Higher Power.

Another surprise move

I still have a postcard that I received from my Polish cousin Henia, signed by several of my classmates when they visited the salt mine Wieliczka on a school field trip.

It's amazing that it reached me as that summer while I was at Scout camp, my parents bought their first house and moved us once more. The house was half of a duplex three houses from the end of the TTC subway line at Keele Street where it was above ground. The noise of squealing brakes was horrendous and lasted late into the night. Our new home was perfectly distanced half way between my new (again) elementary school and my sister's high school. Problem was, each of us had a daily 40 minute walk each way. What I didn't understand was why my elementary school was in the opposite direction to my sister's highschool. Bloor Collegiate Institute had an elementary school right next to it, so why didn't I go there? Instead I was registered at Runnymede Public, which was no closer, and I ended up with the tragedy of being the only person not continuing on to the highschool that everyone else went to.

Next door lived a family of seven but Basia and I were forbidden to associate with them. The family had five children and was on welfare.

Not long after, my father bought a Corvair, very similar to the one his sister had. He also bought an 8mm movie camera. There were many movies taken of the city, but almost none of Basia and I. He continued with his photography and had a small darkroom for developing black and white pictures. Sometime around then we also got a 110 Kodak camera with disposable flash bulbs. We could buy blank and white or color film. The color was a fair bit more expensive and the cost of film and developing it along with the flash bulbs, was prohibitive to us; so it was saved for special occasions.

I started grade 7 at Runnymede Public School in Mrs. Shouldice's 7-3 class in the fall. There were 32 of us. I remember the morning exercises started with singing 'God Save the Queen' - which was the official anthem at this time, and reciting the Lord's Prayer in unison. This was followed by announcements. The focus was strong on cursive writing and spelling. Hours spent looking up words in the dictionary. Geography, science, music and home economics/machine shop, were taught by other teachers in the afternoon.

At recess, we were always outside. The boys usually played handball against the brick wall, while the girls skipped rope. I was quick to learn double dutch and loved it, but never spoke to anyone so I didn't make real friends.

I remember one day in class a boy named Hillary passed me a note telling me that his friend David Payton wanted to take me out on a date. I said yes, and he picked me up and we went to a Saturday matinee. We were both too shy and nervous to speak at all and that was the end of that.

But another boy, a braver one, also had his eye on me. His name was Charlie Cook and I have very fond memories of him. It started when the teacher pushed desks together and we ended up facing front beside each other. One day he scribbled a funny note at the top of a legal size pad (called 'foolscap block' at that time) and slid it over to me. I wrote my reply and slid it back. Being in the front row, Mrs. Shouldice could see what we were doing, but never stopped us. So we continued this until weeks later, she reorganized the class in a different way.

This time my desk was behind his, so instead of notes, Charlie started leaving me candy. I would arrive in class to find red licorice laces on my desk. I would flash a smile at him and mouth a thank you and he would act surprised and grin. Other days it was different treats, but I remember the laces most. His kindness really touched me.

He asked me out and we went to the movies. He'd hold my hand and walk me home, but he lived in the opposite direction and the distance was definitely a deterrent.

Other than that, I spoke to no one. I was the quietest one in the class, but also got the highest marks. The girl that was the loudest and most outspoken, was also the only one that walked the same route as I did. Her name was Livia. This was not a girl that I initially wanted to get to know, as she was quite loud in class and I was intimidated by her. So we walked separately like this for a few months.

At this time, the subway ended a block from our house at Keele Street and there was an exit (but not an entrance) 3 houses from us. There was a streetcar that continued west along Bloor. It cost 10 cents but having a mortgage, I remember my parents only giving me the money on very few occasions. So I walked in the rain, in the snow and in the heat. Eventually that girl and I conceded that we might as well walk together. We soon entertained ourselves by making insignificant wishes on Royal Mail trucks and lucky pennies, and delighted in our magic 'powers' when many of them came true.

My sister and I really wanted to continue playing piano, so one day an upright arrived but unfortunately it was so badly out of tune that it was not possible to use. And there was no money to have it tuned.

We were preparing to spend Christmas Day at Aunt Lidia's house and I expressed the desire to buy gifts for my family. I remember she gave me a couple of dollars and I went to the plaza to see what I could purchase with it. Imagine the joy of a twelve year old girl when she came across the 'party favors' section of the drugstore. I put a lot of thought into choosing something meaningful for each family member and took a great deal of care in wrapping them. On Christmas Eve we stayed home and Christmas came and I remember getting a stuffed blue poodle. I don't know why. Perhaps because I mentioned that I wished we had a dog? And that Christmas Day at Aunt Lidia's, being the youngest member of the family, my excitement to give gifts was greater than receiving them. You guessed it: my effort was not even worthy of acknowledgement, but no matter. I still remember the sense of pride I felt at my initiative and ingenuity.

Chapter 8 - 1967

My father continued to be a very unhappy man. He was now working as a part-time bookkeeper at a Polish newspaper. It was an obvious stop for many Polish immigrants. One of the first questions people asked each other was "Where did you serve?" While his sister was somewhat of a war hero, his experience was not something to be proud of and he didn't care to engage in conversations on this topic. So people found him standoffish and unfriendly. He just wasn't comfortable explaining that he served on the side of the Germans under the naive impression that that would ensure his father's release from the Oranienburg Concentration camp.

My mother still worked at Timex. My parents did not get along and since my mother insisted on separate bedrooms, my sister and I had to share. The only time that we somewhat got along was when we had separate rooms. Unfortunately that didn't happen often. So the solution ended up being that every few months, when things got bad, we alternated. My sister and I would get the two small bedrooms while our parents shared the large master bedroom at the front of the house. Then when their unhappiness grew too large, my sister and I moved into the master, and our parents got the two small bedrooms. Back and forth while we lived in that house.

No love of any kind was ever expressed. Not to us and not by them to each other. If I was around my father, I was told to just stay out of his way, not talk to him and not make any noise as that only bothered people because I had nothing of value to say and nobody was interested. I continued to be a painfully quiet 'wallflower' who apologized for taking up space. Not having anyone else to give me guidance and still seeking my father's approval I also became as much of a tomboy as I could, thinking that would please him. I also was a willing student of chess because that was one of the few things that he was willing to spend time with me on. At age 13, my skills improved sufficiently and I made the mistake of beating him. He refused to play chess with me after that.

I remember little else about our home life, but I cannot forget the arguments, especially as much to my detriment, I was now allowed more time indoors. Never have I known any other person who could carry on an argument by himself. No matter how hard our mother would try to say things to appease him, he would find fault. If she told him he was right on everything, he would find fault with her choice of words or her attitude. Or he would argue the opposite. If she said black, he would argue white. If she said you're right, it was white, he would argue that it was black. She was not allowed to have an opinion or an original thought, but then he would criticize her for not having one. She was damned if she did and damned if she didn't and so were we. A tyrant's methods have crazy making as their goal and he was a master at baiting us into stupid, endless debates. Then if we were foolish enough to express any exasperation or emotion, he would label us as defective. If we shed a tear, we would be labeled 'hysterical' and mentally unsound. Then we would be ordered to smile…

Dad never liked men, nor do I remember him being even friends with any. And because he gushed over, admired and complemented women, the irony was only obvious to the women in his immediate family. So no one knew that he treated us - including his mother but not his sister - with disdain bordering on contempt.

Being such a voracious reader on the subject, he learned that according to the psychiatrist Dr.

Thomas Szasz, early psychiatrists created the diseases of mental illness by classifying certain behaviors that were disturbing to society in general, under the heading of a diagnosis, despite no evidence at the time of a cellular-level disease process. This process was often seen as the manufacture of disease, a sort of large-scale hoax which created and justified the social roles of psychiatrists but were nothing more than a sanctioned form of social control often used by husbands to place their wives in institutions just to be rid of them.

My mother had a healthy fear of this for herself as well as us, and continued to encourage us to remain docile. In future years, most of our extended family believed we were nasty to even say one negative thing about him and thus rejected us.

The beginning of another lifelong friendship

Even though we did not interact at school, Livia and I eventually realized how much easier the walking time was when we walked together. So that is how our 55 year friendship started. She quickly realized how naive I was and elected herself to be my instructor and protector. She talked, I listened, we walked. Fall, winter and spring, we walked.

Since I lived 3 blocks past her house I started to call on her on the way to school. Eventually she asked me to stop in on our way home. Her mom would usually offer us a snack and we would go up to her room. I remember she was very surprised that I did not drink water. In Europe, there was still a memory of water borne diseases so I grew up with the awareness that people drank either juice, hot milk, tea or beer. And never with meals, as that diluted the digestive juices. She shared the front room at 103 Keele St. facing the Keele Street Public School (which only went up to grade 6) with her brother, but it was divided in half. There was no door so her brother would eavesdrop and annoy us. I remember I was occasionally allowed to sleep over at her place, but she was never allowed a night anywhere away from home.

Her house was very different from mine. Her parents had arrived from Italy before she was born and still spoke Italian at home. Or I should say 'yelled' in Italian. I found this very intimidating as I could never tell if they were happy or angry. Her father was an engineer with the city of Toronto and her mother was a very kind stay at home mom, but unable to converse in English. She often invited me to eat with them and sometimes I would be persuaded. I was extremely conscious of 'imposing' on them and it took Livia a long time to convince me that the invitations were sincere. I had my first real italian pizza there. She also drank water and encouraged me to as well, which I found very strange!

Glenlake Park was nearby and we went skating and sledding there.

Church

Her family attended the St. Joan of Arc Catholic Church on Bloor Street and eventually I started to attend as well. My parents didn't show any interest where I went so it was easy for me. Rather than go with her family, Livia and I started to go for the 8a.m. mass alone. On the way home, we often stopped in a convenience store on the corner of Bloor and Keele. I remember my favourite was chocolate popsicles which were 10 cents at this time, and Livia usually treated me as I had no access to money. I also started to go to confession and eventually signed up for confirmation bible classes. All this without my parents knowing. I don't know how, but I asked my aunt Danuta (Magda's mom) to be my sponsor.

The classes were taught by a young priest who, besides teaching us from the Bible, introduced us to the book "The Little Prince". Livia and I wanted to bond by sharing a saint. I had wanted 'Stephanie' but was told there wasn't a St. Stephanie so Livia and I chose the name Beatrice.

This routine was much preferable to spending Sunday mornings listening to my father's 'discussions', which really were monologues and early mass was my way of escaping. When I happened to be home, the hook was the rare attention and hope for approval and the topics were usually about the evils of religion or politics. Basia and I thought that if we just sat at his feet like good little disciples and repeated back to him what we thought he wanted to hear, he would be happy with us. I don't remember it ever working. Each discussion would end with either one of us in tears and dad with that triumphant gloating look of pride that he 'got us' to lose control. I felt shamed and hated myself for being duped yet again. But I could not speak: my throat would lock.

Music

Aunt Lidia convinced dad to buy a black and white television, that it would help us with English. He did and I remember watching a lot of TV. My favourite show was still "The Man from U.N.C.L.E." and I never missed an episode. I learned that David McCallum was a musician. He was my top favorite actor and I was thrilled to acquire a large poster of him to hang on my wall.

Another show that I really liked was Daniel Boone and my favorite actor there was Ed Ames. He played Mingo and I noticed that I gravitated toward actors who were also musicians. His music was another favorite and I got his album next.

The "Man from U.N.C.L.E" spin off "The Girl From U.N.C.L.E." arrived in 1966-7 and I was a loyal fan. Stephanie Powers was a great role model and I quickly adapted her name as my own. Livia and I sent in for membership cards and I chose the name "Mickie Powers" while she chose "Jackie West". We wrote stories with us as main characters.

The other actor on the show was Noel Harrison and I soon discovered that he was also a musician. My favorite song of his was "One of Us Cannot Be Wrong".

We played secret agents as we rode our bicycles with walkie talkies all around the neighbourhood including the roads and ravines of High Park.

Jurek recognized my interest in music and gifted me with a guitar and when he saw that I was an eager student, took the time to teach me to play. And that became my voice. For many years after, I was not seen nor heard without it. I remember the first song I ever learned was "Last Train to Clarksville". The next one was "I'm a Believer", both by the group 'The Monkeys' who also had their own TV show.

Middle School

At school, just like in Poland, the classroom environment was very quiet to enable focus. That is still the only way that I can concentrate when on a task. I have never learned how to ignore or tune out distractions. My children on the other hand, grew up in noisy classrooms and were able to do their homework while listening to music. I think they have a very hard time understanding that I never acquired this ability.

The school offered a trip to middle school students to attend Expo '67 in Montreal. School trips and summer camps were something that I had no trouble persuading my parents for, as long as the cost was low. I remember being disappointed that my best friend Livia was not allowed to come, so I didn't have anyone to pal around with or share memories. I remember we were billeted in the modern Habitat '67 housing. And I remember having a great time and I sent her a postcard. I also remember that we had to learn to sing the 100 year anniversary Canada song as well as the Ontario song. I loved them both.

I was allowed to have a birthday party when I turned 13. This was only my second birthday party ever and I was very excited. Since I only had one friend - Livia - she invited three of her friends to come. The five of us had lunch and cake at my house and then went for a walk to High Park.

As I was a teenager now, Aunt Lidia made me feel very special when she took me shopping downtown. I remember her buying me my first cologne at Sears: Muguet Lilies of the Valley. That was a flower that also grew in her side garden and it became my favourite.

School was coming to an end and Livia, Robert, (who was sweet on Livia) Charlie and I asked our teacher Mrs. Shouldice, to please place us in the same class for grade 8. She assured us that she would do her best. I was excited to bring my report card home, but having the top marks in my class had to be its own reward. The saddest thing was that my father, with his put downs and criticisms, would intentionally take away whatever confidence I earned.

That summer a beagle joined our family. Dad picked it out but unfortunately my sister and I had been hoping for a real dog, like a german shepherd, lab or lassie. So I don't remember how long we had him, his name or what happened to him. Perhaps he was just on loan to us, like the one in Cieszyn?

Polish Scout camp time came again and my cousin Magda has told me that I was entrusted with watching her on the bus ride to Barry's Bay. She was 9 year old and this was her first time to camp. Regretfully, I don't remember whether I did a good job or not, as I had my guitar with me and was busy learning to accompany the singalongs.

Aunt Lidia picked me up from camp and took me to a friend's cottage, where the lady's 8 year old grandson taught me how to fish with worms. I remember having a lot of fun paddling around on an air mattress.

To my surprise, I came home to the same address.

The rest of the summer Livia and I spent in her backyard. They had a large backyard with an above ground pool. A few times we were able to go swimming at the Sunnyside or High Park pool, but that was it.

Livia's 6 year old brother Silvio continued to pester us. He, being a male child, was spoiled and it was difficult to exclude him but he just did not fit in with two 13 year old girls who had just gotten their periods. I got mine without warning or instruction from my mother. She just got a pad and showed me how to strap it on.

I remember they had a sewing room in the basement and that Livia sewed many of her own clothes. I remember watching Star Trek episodes with her family. Livia had great admiration for Mr. Spock while my favourite was Chekov because he reminded me of Illya Kuryakin from Man From U.N.C.L.E. I also remember that like other children, we sometimes made prank calls from her house phone. One of the favourites at that time was "Hello, is your fridge running?" and "Is there a Chester Field in your house?" I spent a fair bit of time at her house that summer, but my quiet and sensitive nature never adjusted to the volume and tension of that Italian household.

Funny thing about phones back then: they were useful, but not addictive or pleasurable. My father was the main person answering the phone in my house and he always used this fake deep baritone voice to say "hello?"

Grade 8

On the first day of school, Livia and I couldn't contain our anxiety, and much to our dismay, we realized we'd been placed in separate classes for grade 8. I was shocked to realize that my diligence backfired. Having the highest marks in the class, I was placed in the 'browner' class with Mr. Sinclair without any of the same classmates from the previous year. Getting top marks felt like a punishment to me now.

As disappointed as I was, it turned out to be my best year in a Canadian school. This was truly an amazing class with an amazing teacher and I eventually made 2 friends: Vera and Rosemary. The other kids had known each other from past years together, and once again I was the only one with the weird accent. Plus the disappointment of losing my newfound social life and potential boyfriend was long lasting.

The curriculum was advanced and unorthodox, starting the day with newspaper headlines, discussing current events and listening to comedian Bill Cosby records. Desks were now grouped, no longer in rows.

Livia and I continued to walk together. I remember one day as we came out of the school gate, there was Charlie smoking with a couple of friends. He smiled and said 'hi'. I really missed him and wanted to stop and chat, but Livia insisted we leave. She lectured me on the way home that because he smoked, he was no good and I was not to have anything more to do with him. I trusted that she knew best so I did as I was told.

The rare time that she was allowed to spend time at my house, we hung out in the basement, playing records and inventing a gymnastics dance routine. I got my first album by then. It was Herman's Hermits and the second was The Monkees.

My father took every opportunity to engage Livia in conversation. He told her how his reason for moving to Canada was to give his daughters a better life with the unlimited opportunities that this free country allowed. He marvelled at how ambitious she was, determined to follow in her father's footsteps for a career in engineering. And he especially admired her aversion to marriage and children.

My father compared me to her for many years into the future, praising her in front of me as well as in private. So I could see that he wasn't incapable of it, it was just me that was defective. He frequently admonished me by saying: "why can't you be more like your friend Livia?" He also was impressed at how outspoken she was, frequently contradicting him. And he would smile and tell her she had a valid point. The ironic thing was that having such an anti-church attitude, he never held it against her that she was a devoted Catholic!

It was all very confusing to me: if I acted like that, I was punished. No other person, hell: not even communism!, took away my freedom of speech like he did. This carried on for the rest of my life.

The winter of 1967 was another particularly harsh one with four-five foot snow drifts, freezing temperatures and high humidity which leaves you feeling colder still. I remember asking my father for a dime to ride the streetcar and being told that no, that every penny was needed to pay the mortgage. I resented his focus on money. Even more now that I had started getting my period and usually the first day or two, I would have a heavy flow with severe cramps. Some days I stayed home as not being able to face the long walk was bad enough but what was even worse, was that in the mid '60's, girls were not allowed to wear pants at school. And the menstrual pads were not sticky with wings: instead, they were attached to a thin elastic belt with clips. This contraption had a bad habit of shifting and therefore leaking. There was no worse embarrassment for a thirteen year old.

The number one priority for my father and by extension, my mother - since she never contradicted anything he said - was to buy a house and pay off the mortgage as soon as possible, no matter what sacrifice it entailed. And the sacrifice was my sister's and mine well being. As much as he liked to tell people that he moved us to Canada to give his daughters the opportunity for a better life, it was far from the truth. When he picked the location of his first, second and third houses, they could not have been further from the nearest schools. Not once, but three times.

For the next five years I had 40 minute walks each way, rain, snow or bitter cold: even though the streetcar stop was less than 100 feet away, I was repeatedly denied the 10 cents it would cost for me to take it.

His goal of paying off their mortgage meant that every penny went towards it. We did without so much, that we actually had LESS basic creature comforts than in poverty stricken communist Poland. Or perhaps it just felt like less, since we now had a different scale of comparison around us.

Chapter 9 - 1968

It was spring, I was 13 years old and doing really well in Mr. Sinclair's class; and playing guitar every spare moment after. A boy named Steven in my class who also played guitar suggested we perform on stage during a school dance, between the DJ sets. We did a couple of songs together and I did one on my own. I remember it was 'To Sir With Love'. Dedicated to our teacher. This was a highlight for me and increased my confidence.

My mother did something wonderful for me: she sewed me a cream colored dress with fringes, just like one that I saw Susan Jacks had. It had long sleeves with the fringe running down the back of them, a fringe across the back, and a shirt collar with a 'u' shape split front decorated with fringe. And to top it off, I got a pair of white go-go boots. I loved that dress and wish that I had a picture of it. I also wish I had worn it for graduation. Instead I was influenced to wear a gray dress that Aunt Lidia bought me, and my hair was cut shorter. I failed to speak up for myself.

In the winter we went skiing just outside Toronto at Albion Hills, where there was a rope pull. I remember I had a long tuque that doubled up as a scarf.

Three people escaped from Czechoslovakia and since two of them were distant family, my aunt Livia took them in. Michael was my father and Lidia's 3rd cousin, descended from one of the Sikora sisters whose name was Ewa and she had married into the Walach family. He arrived with his wife Alena and his best friend Zbycho. I remember they came to visit us several times. I remember when he and Alena would come to visit, she would stay downstairs while he came upstairs into my room to play chess with me. He was 21. How could that not look wrong to my parents?

I was 14 and enjoyed the attention. He complimented me and took an interest in what I thought about. He would encourage me to dream about things that I wanted and we would bet these things on the chess game. As all celebrations were still held at Lidia's we also ran into this couple there. He was always very happy to see me. I had gotten into the habit of sitting on the floor, out of the way, being seen but not heard, while the adults smoked and debated various topics. Usually, after ten or so minutes, Michael would come and sit by me. He would tell me that he found me more interesting to talk to while I gravitated towards anyone that gave me the slightest bit of approval, encouragement or attention that I was so desperately lacking from my parents. And amazingly, no one stopped his access to me. Not once. Though my mother displayed intense disapproval of my behavior I don't remember my father objecting. Looking back, I think he had a twisted disconnect. He was way too attracted to young women himself, and probably was happy to have Alena's attention all on him.

Not long before this my sister went out on a date with a boy named Jim Williams. She was 16 and he was 22. Mother told him not to call ever again. Broke my sister's heart and she never forgave her for that. So why didn't mother tell Michael off? Was it because he was married and related to us so therefore no threat in her eyes? Or was I just not valuable enough to protect? Or did my father's enjoyment of Alena's visits take priority?

Two days after my 14th birthday, Livia's baby sister Julie was born. Livia was put in charge of her care and much of our time together came to an end. Due to this, she vowed that she would never get married or have children. A cousin had arrived from Italy and was living with them as well. We started to drift apart.

But the most painful reason was about to become apparent. Even though we had been two years in the same house, I was forced to change schools because of district boundaries. And we lived one block on the wrong side for grade 9. I had been at Runnymede Public School for two years and though I had only made 3 friends in that time, I was gaining confidence. I expected to continue into highschool with familiar faces. Imagine my shock when I was told that I would not be attending the same highschool as everyone else because Keele Street was the boundary and I lived one street further. And that put me outside of the boundary for Humberside Collegiate and a 45 minute walk in the opposite direction. I begged my parents to intervene but to no avail.

Graduation from elementary school came and summer followed. This year, my father decided to take the family and drive me to camp and some three hours later, after the long trip in a hot car, we were there. Upon arriving several days early at the region called Kaszuby near Barry's Bay, all my sister and I wanted to do was jump in the lake and cool off but my father insisted that the car had to be unpacked, tent set up and dinner made. Needless to say, by the time all that was done, it was too dark to swim. I remember he punished us for sulking.

But Scout camp was wonderful as always. I was in troop '*Rzeka*' which means river. My cousin Jurek was visiting his girlfriend Dorothy's family cottage there and picked me up one day for a visit. There, I was introduced to music by The Beatles.

This was the year where we were each challenged to spend a night alone in the woods. I knew how to build a shelter, but I didn't really see the point. My main concern was that if an animal came near me during the night, I would not be able to scare it off as I had this strange inability to yell. Basically, I couldn't (and still can't) yell. I can raise my voice to a certain degree, maybe just enough to call someone from a few yards away, but you're rarely going to hear me outright scream. I like singing, but my voice is weak because I can't belt out certain notes.

Me reacting to pain is a very low pitched groan or gasp at most. Or just my mouth opening with no sound at all. I never learned how to *actually* yell or scream, because I was never allowed to.

In the fall, with a feeling of severe discouragement, I started grade 9 at Bloor C.I. The school had over 3,000 students and I was lost and alone once again. I felt out of place in this new school with a high mixture of different nationalities: loud and boisterous people. It was a shock to be all alone again. Most of the kids had gone to Kent Elementary and already had established friendships.

Apart from my sister, I knew no one. This was the first time that she and I attended the same school, but being in grade 11, she was not happy about me being only two years behind her now, and I felt that she went out of her way to avoid me. Perhaps it's not true but I have no memory of any interaction with her. And so I made every effort to be different. She never left home without makeup, stockings and heels. She curled her hair. She was blond and seemed so confident. She flirted with boys. So I wore knee socks and shunned femininity in order to cope with her rejection. And I continued to be invisible.

Again, I felt that I was penalized for my high marks as I was automatically streamed into the 5 year Arts and Science curriculum leading to university. The friends that I eventually made in that first year of highschool were all in the 4 year business program. Dea Brusco, my second closest friend, was Italian as well. How I envied the business students. I wanted to learn typing and shorthand, as that would be extremely useful for transcribing songs from the radio.

Living in a rooming house

Shortly after, my parents sold our house and bought a large brick 4 level rooming house at 124 Westminster Avenue in the heart of the Polish district of Toronto and we moved again. At this location there was no convenient way to catch the subway or streetcar to school, but the location reduced my walk by a whole 5 minutes.

The house had 6 bedrooms. Our kitchen and small living room were in the dark damp basement. The main level front room originally meant to be the living room was rented out to a tall, stately, mid-30's lady named Lucynka. With her bleached blond hollywood hairstyle, she was like a southern belle. Several years later, she ended up marrying a Polish man named Bodgan who was a foot shorter than her and balding, and who had courted her there. I remember he had a big car and had trouble seeing over the steering wheel! He could have been a double for the actor Wallace Shawn, who played Vizzini in 'The Princess Bride'.

In the back, my father converted the dining room into their bedroom. There were three bedrooms, a small kitchen and a bathroom on the second floor. One was rented to a German lady named Elfie who worked at Timex with my mother. She drove a white Opel sports car. The middle room was occupied by a petite dark haired girl in her 20's who worked as a stewardess. She was quite friendly to me and let me hang out in her room when my sister complained about my non stop guitar playing. My parents frequently chastised me for bothering the tenants but this girl seemed to enjoy having me around.

The room at the front was rented by a couple recently arrived from Poland, Jerzy and Ala Pohler. She was beautiful and fun loving and my father was smitten. Didn't he connect that he had two daughters who were easy prey for creepy attention like he was doing? I remember dad lent them $5,000 and took a painting as collateral. They ghosted him and he never got over it.

Then it was cousin Ewa from Sweden and Mariola before mother finally put her foot down. He couldn't have been more impressed with each and every one of them. In comparison, my sister and I felt like Cinderellas. Not a compliment was ever sent in our direction from his lips. And now there was plenty of work, laundry with a wringer washer was not an easy task, and we did not have a dryer. The push lawn mower was also our responsibility.

The top floor had two bedrooms. The front one housed an elderly gentleman, quiet and respectful, who came as part of the package with the house purchase. The back bedroom was for my sister and I. Fortunately the bedroom was large enough to divide in two, and our father agreed to build the wall. The window was in the center of the room opposite the door, so it kinda worked. The only thing that could not be fixed, was the entry. I had to step two feet into her portion in order to enter my room on the right. Why she didn't get my side where a door could be put in, I don't know.

I set about decorating, painting and sewing curtains and bedding: I finally had a space that I didn't have to share. But first I needed to earn some money, and that opportunity came when I made friends with a girl who lived across the street, named Elizabeth Plachetsky. We were great friends for a while and roamed the neighborhood. We biked to the High Park swimming pool. I played guitar on the front porch and we sang, especially when Billy, the pharmacy delivery boy passed by on his route. We serenaded him with the current hit

"Which Way You Goin Billy" but he hardly ever looked our way.

She introduced me to a young couple a few houses down from ours who had a 6-8 month old baby. Since they usually went out after putting the baby to sleep, I had very little to do besides washing dishes and tidying up the kitchen. And there, I came across my first encounter with Playboy magazine. The pictures were quite modest by today's standards but I still couldn't believe my eyes. My first view of the male anatomy was a bit of a shock.

This house also had several tenants and one in particular was determined to catch my eye. He was 16, wore cowboy boots and shirts with snaps and lived with his older brother. He was from eastern Canada and had a job. I don't remember his name, as I was not allowed to date him. The reason? He invited me out to a restaurant for a Coke, and that was, for an unknown reason, off limits. Or so I was told.

I felt proud to have my first babysitting job and earn some spending money. I saved up enough for my first purchase of fabric, with which I made curtains and a bedspread for my room. The colors were bold: burnt oranges and browns and I remember seeing a fleeting look of approval on my father's face. This was confirmed years later when he decorated their house in Kelowna with similar color and patterned curtains. These curtains also hung in their condo: their final independent residence.

Elizabeth and I continued to roam. The lake and beach were close, as were the stores and a different Catholic Church. Livia and I had drifted apart by now and attending early morning mass with her at St. Joan of Arc was no longer an option. One day a man in a pickup truck called us over for directions. Or so he said. With Elizabeth at one window and I at the other, he didn't know who to charm as he was stroking himself. We raised our eyebrows towards each other and burst out laughing. He drove away. It never occurred to us to report him and we were not traumatized. There was absolutely zero chance that we were in any danger. At 14, we had street smarts and knew how to look after ourselves.

Chapter 10 - 1969

Christmas came and went and besides receiving another Christmas card, letter and *Opłatek* from Janusz and his family, the highlight was that my father agreed to a snowmobile rental. It was a rare day of fun: I'm not sure what we did to deserve it. Perhaps not complaining about the clothes he picked out and brought home for my sister and I at Salvation Army and Honest Ed's? My sister never wore what he bought so he eventually gave up on her. But I was still determined to win his approval. I remember in particular an oversized olive green shapeless winter jacket that I had to wear. He also bought many books as well as anything in teak and leather. On most Saturday mornings he headed downtown to shop and that was that.

My worst nightmare came true when I awoke one morning with a mouthful of shattered teeth. It was an unimaginable shock for a 14 year old. I've blocked out most of that time as I was fitted with some sort of plastic caps.

In the spring our school choir headed to Rochester, NY for a music exchange with a highschool there. I don't remember much about it except that on the way back, having a couple of dollars in my pocket, I splurged on a souvenir bean bag lion and named her Sally. My daughter claimed it at two years old and my granddaughter has it now.

My cousin Jurek and his girlfriend took me to an outdoor Janice Joplin concert in downtown Toronto. I remember it being summer as we sat on a blanket on the grass.

Apart from watching TV, music was my passion and by this time I had also become a big fan of going to see a live theatre with Noel Harrison and Mitzi Gaynor and meeting them afterward.

Sneaking into the Royal York Hotel and exploring all the way up to the attic all afternoon was another highlight. Knowing how to make myself 'invisible' had its advantages!

Scout camp

Along with my guitar, I was once again put on the scout bus and sent off for a month to this survival training camp which cost my parents a mere $25. I truly, deeply loved going.

The girls and boys' camps were separated by significant distances. That year our troop was called

'*Zarzewie*', which means embers. The first task, once again, was setting up the old and heavy canvas tents. I remember we dug trenches around each perimeter to keep the rain from seeping underneath. There were wooden pallets set on the ground inside, and on those, four to a tent, we placed our air mattresses and sleeping bags. The second, as in past years, was digging the latrines. The spots were designated, the instructions given and the shovels handed out. A six by three hole needed to be dug, six feet deep. The two seater wooden huts were waiting. Everyone rotated on kitchen duty as well.

I sent a postcard to Livia telling her that when I arrived *"my uniform was in such ghastly condition that it was condemned by the leaders and sent to another camp for ironing."* (Livia still has the postcard)

Our camp was located on the edge of one of the lakes and we had kayaks. We also swam almost daily. I remember when I almost drowned. I stepped off an underwater ledge and went under without the chance to fill my lungs with air. No one noticed. I struggled for what seemed like an eternity and finally touched bottom and was able to rebound. What I remember was trying to suppress my gasping for air so that I would not attract attention and cause a scene. Other than to my spiritual guides,

I was too embarrassed to call for help. Parental words persist even in the threat of death...my second close call.

Guard duty was the most exciting as well as scary. In pairs, we did four hour shifts from sundown to sunup. We were responsible to sound the alarm in the event of a raid by another camp. If we failed, our tent pegs were pulled out and our flag stolen.

There was much marching and singing. I had made a point of memorizing some jokes as a way to make friends and it worked. I made friends and because the camp operated in the Polish language, I was one of the few who was admired for speaking it so fluently.

All the troops gathered around huge campfires. Many large and small sing-a-longs. One in particular stands out where my friend Regina and I sang. We had chosen the popular song "House of the Rising Sun" and got an unexpected ovation in return. It was done by another troop, by way of serenading us with the "Light My Fire" song. This was another highlight in my life that I'll never forget.

A couple of dances in a nearby hall. I remember enjoying the music even though I was never asked to dance. Outdoor Sunday services. I really enjoyed these but for some reason had trouble staying awake. One time I volunteered for flag duty at the front but that turned out to be more difficult because I was still very sleepy and if I dozed off, I would fall down. Sometimes I volunteered to stay behind and do kitchen duty for lunch in order to avoid the potential embarrassment.

Afterwards, my father arrived with Michael and Zbycho to pick us up. My love of horses continued and I remember persuading my father to let Basia and I go horseback riding. Michael and Zbycho came as well and Zbycho's head hit a branch at a gallop and he fell off, luckily with only a headache. Mother found out and we got caught hell from her. Later on, as we sat on the ground by the campfire, I snuggled up to Michael and fell asleep in front of him.

Back at home, my father brought visitors home. A woman with her two sons had just defected from Poland. The older one mesmerized me. His name was Julek Gamski and he was my age. He had records with him and the music of these Polish groups reawakened in me feelings of homesickness. How could he be so confident and happy when being recently uprooted? I assume that like my sister, he was at the age of craving travel and adventure. I hung on his every Polish word.

His mother started a Polish folk dancing group in the Catholic Church on Roncesvalles and I was thrilled to join. I also attended Scout meetings at that location. The thrill of that time was increased when I learned that the Polish band '*Skaldowie*' came to Toronto for a concert. It turned out Julek had met them on the ship Batory coming over, and I not only got to meet them but also got an autograph.

He also introduced me to his friend Bogdan Gawronski and his sister, and I introduced them to my neighbor Elizabeth. Summer was a dream, roaming the neighbourhood and hanging out with the two Elizabeths, Bodgan and Julek, playing music on my front porch. I don't think any of them set foot in our house. I remember it being a serious imposition if I invited anyone in, even for a brief visit. If he was in the living room, father would glare at us from behind his newspaper or else leave the room with a dramatic huff. I rarely invited anyone over, and anyway, my friends never wanted to come back for a second visit.

I did what I could to fulfill my need for friendship, stability and belonging. Even though our house was filled with strangers living in rented rooms and I wasn't at any closer distance to school, I was optimistic.

A few months later they were gone. Moved to England to join his father where Julek formed a band that he plays in to this day.

Grade 10 started that September. My friend Dea, being in the four year program, was now taking business classes. How I wished I also could, mainly because typing and shorthand would have come in very handy for writing songs out. She also loved to sing and sometimes came by my house to sit and sing on the porch.

I remember losing my interest to excel at school. More and more I noticed that if my sister or I brought home a test with an A- mark, my father would look up from behind his newspaper and say: "I'm disappointed in you; why didn't you get an A or A+? You didn't study hard enough". We were growing up with a parent who expected perfection and we were criticized heavily when we didn't live up to that expectation. Perfection became one of my false core values and in hindsight continued to plague me the rest until now as I write this.

I finally realized that I could never do well enough to get the attention and approval that I craved so much. I started to give up and let my schoolwork slide. And teachers who made it their policy to never give perfect marks for anything, certainly didn't help.

Do we choose our parents so that we can remember to learn what our soul needs to learn?

It amazes me that neither Basia nor I was not one of the statistics of immigrant girls turning to drugs and prostitution as a way to escape family tyranny and unreasonable expectations. There were many such girls on Yonge Street downtown and in Yorkville. And many of these girls in those days had circumstances less severe than ours. I did some foolish things and on occasion found myself in sketchy situations, but I am sure that my guardian angels were watching over me and I was sensitive enough to hear them and smart enough to listen to them. Besides; I was not a quitter and I refused to become a predictable statistic.

Twenty years later, I beat the odds again while raising my three children as a single mother.

I don't know why it felt like we lived there for a long time, but two months into grade 10, my father sold the house and with very little notice, we moved to the outskirts of Toronto suburbs. While I was happy in our rooming house, my sister tells me that she was unhappy that the house was too embarrassing to bring friends home and I imagine there were financial reasons as well. The house was under constant renovation and I don't think the rents were enough to cover the costs. My father was still working only part time at the small Polish newspaper office. My mother continued to be the main breadwinner with her job at Timex. I remember we each got a new wrist watch every couple of years.

It was October and I remember doing quite badly in chemistry so that was the only reason that I didn't mind the move. The other was that we were moving to an apartment complex and there would be a swimming pool. So the decision was made to move us up to 10 Parkway Forest Drive in Willowdale, near to the newly built Fairview Mall. To get to school, I now had to cross the bridge over the 401, a walk which took about 20 minutes each way. George S. Henry Secondary School was smack in the middle of a wealthy neighbourhood with an exclusive golf club.

The transfer to my new highschool was challenging. While my sister, who was at this time in grade 12, was able to stay at Bloor, I was not. Once again, new neighborhood, new students, new routine. There was no choir so in order to continue with music, I had to pick a band instrument. Being 2 months into the school year, there were no choices left and I was stuck with a clarinet. We did not get along. Mathematics and French continued to be my favorite subjects and I developed skills in phys ed. My teacher wrote that my gymnastics routine was "almost first class" and that my skill in badminton was above average.

Shortly after I arrived, the geography class was scheduled for a week-long field trip to Caledon Hills and not knowing anyone, I took my guitar for company.

"Albion Hills Field Centre is a beautiful experiential learning facility nestled within a scenic conservation park in Caledon, ON. teaching outdoor, nature-based programs."

We did cartography, studied biology and played outdoor games. One game was very similar to the one I played in Poland. Two teams, trying to infiltrate the terrain and without getting tagged, steal the other team's flag in the dark. Hot chocolate, music and much exciting conversation followed.

So that's how I met Peter, who it turned out, was captain of the junior football team. He had strawberry blond hair and an easy smile. It was wonderful to have a boyfriend at Christmas time and I remember my mother helping me to knit a pair of gloves for him. They were red and white and had a nordic snowflake pattern. His family belonged to the golf and country club and I remember being included in several family dinners there.

Peter had wonderful parents and two older brothers. His mother accepted me with love. But due to peer pressure, he just couldn't stop pressuring me to engage in more than just kissing. He would get much too intense and I just wasn't ready. The joy of having a boyfriend, especially such a popular one soon wore off, as I spent most of our time together fighting off this sweaty boy and it just stopped being fun.

One day I was invited to his house for a dinner celebration as his older middle brother had just returned from a trip to Eastern Europe. I was enthralled and realized that I had so much more in common with him. As much as I was embraced by this family and would have loved to have belonged with them, I realized that it just could not be. I broke it off with Peter.

But there was a guitar club. I remember walking into the room and meeting several people there. One was Susan Pritchard, a buxom blonde who loved to sing but did not play an instrument and Lloyd Summerfield, who would become a dear friend. Soon he invited Sue and I to his house where we started a band. His brother Marvin who was several years older played drums and sometimes joined us. Marv worked for his father's company, Southam Publishing. He also had a younger sister Melissa, called Missy.

There was all kinds of musical equipment as well as a snooker table in the basement. We had great fun, learning songs and harmonizing. Lloyd had a pair of cowboy boots and loved Johnny Cash. I remember many hours spent in his room listening to cassettes.

He also wrote songs, even some for me. One that especially stands out was called "Rini Come Over". Sadly they soon made me uncomfortable as I didn't feel anything to match his growing adoration for me. He was a year younger than I, too short, and had a quick temper. His road rage was most concerning. But his talent as a musician was a gift and his voice could double for the lead singer of the band 'Edward Bear' which was just rising in popularity. In fact, they played at our school once.

Sometimes we performed during lunch hour in the cafeteria. Sue was the lead vocalist and played the tambourine. I loved playing rhythm guitar to Lloyd's lead and singing harmony.

Sue repeatedly failed to 'corrupt' me, encouraging me to use some swear words as well as smoke. And surprisingly my father never tried to impress her and   I was quickly discouraged from bringing her home. We'd barely walk in the door and he was folding his newspaper and moving to his bedroom, with barely a scowl as acknowledgement.

Michael and Alena's daughter Michelle Nicole was born on December 24. I remember we were all gathered at Lidia's when the call came. It was very exciting. As per tradition, we stayed up and played board games till way past midnight. Jurek introduced us to Monopoly. And as per tradition, I once again received a Christmas card with an '*Opłatek*' from Janusz.

Chapter 11 - 1970

It was 1970 and on January 7th, my family was granted Canadian citizenship. I think we went to an office at city hall and recited the pledge of allegiance there. I found it interesting that I could become a Canadian. If any of my friends moved to Poland, they could never become Polish. No matter where you move in the world, I don't think you can ever become that nationality except in Canada and the United States.

Being around baby Michelle gave me a profound sense of joy. I loved helping to take care of her and realized that more than anything, I wanted to be a mother when I grew up. Apart from babysitting Michelle, I also posted a notice in our building. The money I made was spent on guitar lessons. Music was my lifeline, my comfort, my escape as well as a way to connect with people. I wanted to become really good and Jurek recommended an excellent guitar teacher who would take me to another level by teaching me how to finger pick. The one song that he taught me, that stands out in my memory was "Scarborough Fair". I would take the bus there each week - not once was I driven anywhere. My parents were busy being grownups, and if I wanted to go somewhere or do something, I was on my own. That suited me fine as by this time, I was quite capable of earning enough for lessons and bus fare.

But that did not suit my father and soon I became the target of intensified criticism. He said that I spent too much time on playing and should strive to be more well rounded: a 'jill-of-all-trades'. Hence, I was forbidden to continue.

And so I switched to judo. I researched it, and signed myself up for classes. I remember one of the junior blackbelts was the Canadian champion. I was so proud when I got my yellow belt and on my way home, I climbed the fence surrounding the outdoor apartment pool and jumped in, in my clothes. It was 10pm. When I came up in the elevator, I heard voices in the hallway. There at our door stood a policeman. My parents had reported me missing, though I was only 15 minutes late. And that was the end of judo.

Not once was I offered a ride, no matter how far or how late I had to travel. It was my full responsibility to arrange and pay for any interests that I pursued. And as soon as I became excited and half way competent, I was forced to quit. He would not allow me to be 'obsessed' as he called it.

Saturday mornings he still went to town to do the rounds of Salvation Army and Honest Ed's and occasionally catch a matinee. My mother, sister and I would clean the house and actually have a bit of fun in his absence. We put music on and even sang. If we neglected to shut it all down before he walked in the door, we were severely rebuked. He called us 'histeryczki' which meant that we were out of control and emotionally unstable. He continued his threats of having my mother committed to a psychiatric institution. Husbands ridding themselves of wives via the psychiatric institution had ceased to be possible since the 1960's but my mother did not know that.

In any troubled relationship between the powerful and the less powerful, like the relationship between a husband and wife in a patriarchal society, the language and ideas of psychiatry and mental health practice are open to abuse as a form of social control.

Though my mother continued being the primary breadwinner and got a promotion to supervisor of the Timex repair department my father was the one that decided how every penny was to be spent. She would hand the paychecks to him and he would put them into a bank account that was solely in his name. In fact, she did not have her name on their bank account until 2006. I know this for a fact, because I was there when she made her first withdrawal. Being in authority came naturally to her and she was much liked and well respected at work. Yet at home, she was powerless and she couldn't figure out why. This made her frustrated and over time hardened her heart.

And so my mother struggled with recurrent depression, migraines and stomach issues, and my sister and I continued to peel potatoes when we got home. We were never taught how to cook: when I asked to help, my mother would say that she could do it better and quicker by herself. Besides the daily ritual of peeling potatoes, the only other kitchen chore that we were trusted with was washing and drying the dishes.

I continued my friendship with Lloyd and we continued to jam. His dream after highschool was for him and I to do the coffee houses and lounges circuit as a duo. I didn't think we'd have a chance but it was fun practicing. His ulterior motive was that we do this as a couple and eventually get married and my rational mind contemplated that as an option, but could not reconcile the inevitable difference in our religions. His mother Paula was a wise, funny, tender, and kindhearted woman. I will never forget her many kindnesses, but I just couldn't see myself converting to Judaism.

Driving lessons

I was excited about turning 16 and finally getting my driver's licence. My father however, wasn't keen on teaching me how to drive. The one time that he allowed me behind the wheel, I scratched the side of the bulky, automatic BelAir as well as the car next to it, while reversing into our parking spot. I left a note and the experience cost me $75. Had my father been the sole influence on me, the consequence of that would have crippled me.

But he wasn't and so it didn't. Instead, I got crippled in a different way.

Fathers must love their daughters well, or else they'll be at risk of being groomed. I was not only not protected, I was blamed for the attention that I was getting. I remember a party at Michael and Alena's apartment where Michael was drunk and trying to steal a kiss when he cornered me in the kitchen. Other times he found ways to persuade me, a 15 year old, to sit on his lap.

He found other ways to keep me hooked. He and Alena bought a brand new orange Ford Maverick and he promised me that he would give me driving lessons. He was my father's cousin. My parents trusted him. I was now spending a fair bit of time at their apartment helping with baby Michelle and assisting with vehicle maintenance. I learned how to change the oil, a flat tire and how to rebuild a carburetor. He told me that the only way to learn to drive was on a standard shift.

And theory was covered in one crucial instruction: "assume every other driver is a blind idiot and you can only ever be happily surprised." I passed this advice to my children and it's kept them safe so far!

The deal Michael offered me was that I was to be ready and waiting downstairs by 7am, every morning for four weeks. If I neglected to be ready on time even once, there would be no second chance. At the end of the four weeks he would take me for my driving test. If I failed, I would owe him dinner at any restaurant of his choice. If I passed, he would buy me breakfast at McDonald's.

The lessons in the near new, sporty Maverick were intimidating but what a joy. The first week, he taught me to shift gears from the passenger seat. I was also to light his cigarettes and pass them to him while he drove. The second week he put me in the driver's seat and shifted gears while I focused on using the clutch and steering. Most of this driving took place on the nearby Don Valley Parkway and the 401 freeway. In his opinion learning to drive in a parking lot was for small children.

By the third week, I was focusing on coordinating the clutch and the gear shift myself. The fourth week was spent on parallel parking and starting on steep hills without stalling or rolling back.

These lessons lasted an hour at which time I was dropped off at school. Four weeks later, I passed my driving test with flying colors and true to his promise, I was rewarded with a MacDonald's breakfast.

My confidence found other sources of encouragement and grew in spite of the situation at home. For my sixteenth birthday, Jurek had given me a fringed doe skin poncho. Unbelievable present that I treasured well into my thirties even though I had little occasion to wear it. Aunt Lidia introduced me to tampons. My mother was horrified and told me that I would be mortified if the tampon fell out and I'd have a red pool on the floor beneath me.

I was now able to persuade my parents to let me have the $16 government baby bonus allowance so that I could start buying my own clothes like my sister could since she turned 16. I remember saving up for my first purchase of three pairs of hip hugger, bell bottom, thin wale corduroy H.I.S. jeans at the Levi store on Yonge Street. I bought one in each available color: black, tan and brown.

Summer came and because I lived too far now to attend any Scout meetings, camp was out of the question. And somehow in the move, my uniform went missing. I would have loved to at least keep my Scout cross, but that too was nowhere to be found. I was sentimental whereas my parents were not.

Instead of camp, I was ready for my first real job. Michael's wife Alena managed a Hilton Stauffer Reducing Salon, which was a popular weight loss chain based on a gimmick. I had to wear a black leotard and show the fat ladies how to do sit ups. However most of them preferred that I set the timer while they put on the vibrating belts or just lay on the vibrating tables. The other girls and I would laugh as we watched some of them treat themselves at the ice cream parlor afterwards. I remember I was making minimum wage: $1.43 per hour.

In grade eleven, being at a highschool in a wealthy and progressive area, a new class called 'Computer Science' was offered and I quickly signed up. I was good at math and the whole concept fascinated me. It consisted of making flow charts then punch cards which produced simple printed banners consisting of letters and numbers. I also pulled my marks up to the 80's in physics, geography, English and French. Through various career testing, my I.Q of 138 was established. With some guidance and encouragement Basia and I would have both gone to university.

Chapter 12 - 1971

It was 1971 and I was still at George S. Henry for grade 11 and I now went by Rene. Lloyd continued to pursue me. I agreed to go to a dance as his date and he took me shopping for a dress. It was mostly red and black, with a bit of white, floor length and not something that I would have picked, but it turned out to be a favorite.

Apart from working Saturdays at the reducing salon, I also continued to babysit in my building. The family had two young daughters and the father was a police officer and an avid photographer, so I didn't hesitate when he asked if he could take some photos of me. His wife was present as he took several pictures of me in the dress that Lloyd had chosen for me. My confidence was boosted.

One day, driving down the Don Valley Parkway with Michael at the wheel of his Maverick, was the third time that I came close to death. It is still as clear in my memory as if it was yesterday. He was speeding in the right lane and all of a sudden a truck pulled in from the feeder lane. Michael slammed on the brakes and the car went into a spin, zigzagging across all three lanes. It was a miracle that on that busy road, not one car hit us. When it finally came to a stop, the Maverick ended up facing traffic. Michael deftly turned it the needed 180 degrees, and we proceeded on our way. He joked to laugh it off while I was speechless, calm and I felt invincible.

March 21-27, I was chosen to attend the week-long music program at the Elliot Lake Centre for Continuing Education. Well known teachers in music, dance and art were there. I remember Andre Gagnon was one of them. I was in the guitar program and the most difficult song I learned to fingerpick there was Leonard Cohen's "Suzanne".

Locals were free to participate in the workshops and this is where I met 17 year old Jimmy Morningstar, an Ojibway native from nearby Blind River. He reminded me of the main character Wabi in the first book I ever read about Canada, 'The Wolf Hunters'.

Scott

But the greatest story of my teen years was meeting Scott on my 17th birthday.

I remember wearing a cream color, crochet hot pants suit that day. I think it was a hand-me-down from Basia that originally had long pants that we cut short. Surprisingly our father didn't say anything when we started to wear mini skirts and hot pants.

Our school was getting an addition; a new gym was being built across from the library. I was changing classes and stopped in the hallway which had windows right next to the building site, as the gym access would be right opposite the library. And there were a half dozen or so workmen pouring and smoothing the new concrete floor. One immediately stood out and I was as if stricken by a thunderbolt. This intense feeling of recognition overcame me. "I know you" raced through my mind as my heart leapt with joy. "You're here and I recognize you!" I screamed inwardly. But outwardly, all I could do was stare as I stood there transfixed.

He looked up from troweling, straightened up, leaned on the long handle, caught my gaze and held it. It wasn't long before the comments started. The other workmen started the teasing as he beamed the most amazing smile at me. All I wanted to know was his name and I would die happy. So that's what I said: "I just want to know his name!" Before anyone responded, this gorgeous dark haired man standing astride on a plank on the wet cement in the middle of the new gym floor, deftly flipped the trowel around and reaching as far as he could, wrote the letters S C O T T in the wet cement. He wrote them so that I could read them. I was speechless, unlike his co-workers.

The bell rang and jolted me out of my reverie. I hurried off to my next class.

At the end of the day, I returned to the window on the right to savor the memory of that magic moment. There was no one in sight and the floor was once again smooth. The cement finishers were done and that was it. Then I heard scraping just under the open window. I looked out and there he was. On his knees, pretending to trowel. He saw me and beamed that smile again. "I want your phone number," he said. I was shaking and couldn't speak. I wrote my phone number on a small piece of paper ripped from my binder and quickly hurried off.

For the next three days I would rush home and eagerly hover near the telephone not daring to let anyone else answer. It took him three days to get the courage up to call a girl whose name he did not know. Finally, the call came: "Hello, This is Scott", he said. "Hi Scott", it's Rini. I'm so glad you called.

He took me out several times, and other times we spent time by the swings in the complex. He lived downtown and drove a light blue mini Cooper. It was a bit funny seeing this 20 year old six foot tall man fold himself into this little car, but I didn't care. Other times he would pick me up from school in his boss' pickup truck. I was so very happy. Every moment of being with him was a bonus. I had never had such a strong feeling of deja vu, of being on the verge of remembering another life, as I did when with him. He taught me to hold a gaze. How important it was to look people in the eye. We would have frequent staring contests and he would let me win. But I made progress. He also taught me how to kiss. Sensuously and lovingly. But that's as far as it would go. He refused to teach me further. When he was with me, he only had eyes for me. Not even my sister could distract him which made me infinitely happy. He filled my ears with sweet nothings which gave me the feelings that made my heart soar with joy.

I left for a two week French exchange trip to Quebec City in July, living with a family in the old part of town. I was starting to think and dream in

French. As well as a postcard to Livia, I responded to Scott's letters. My greatest regret is that years later, I let him convince me to throw away those beautiful love letters. And what a happy reunion we had when I returned! But all too brief.

He told me that his ex-girlfriend who had left him, found out he had moved on and since she hadn't, she demanded that since he took her virginity, she was going to hold him to his promise to marry her.

I remember it was August and we were sitting in his car outside my building and once again my life was summed up in a crying song. This time it was Donny Osmond who spoke:

"Go away little girl,

Go away little girl,

I'm not supposed to be alone with you

I know that your lips are sweet

But our lips must never meet

I'm dating somebody else and I must be true.

Oh, go away little girl

Go away little girl

It's hurting me more each minute that we delay

When you're near me like this

You're much too hard to resist

So go away little girl before I beg you to stay."

And also that he didn't think that he was good enough for me as he had a juvenile criminal record from when he was 16 and he and his friend Tom had got caught breaking into some cottages.

The indoctrination that my father had instilled in me remained strong: "everyone else has life figured out and knows what they're doing. You're the only one that has much to learn, so if people don't want you, you'd best assume that it's your fault." So broken-hearted and with my mother's encouragement, I let him go. The popular message I got from society around me was

> "If you love someone, set them free.
> If they come back they're yours;
> if they don't they never were."

I was naive and knew of no way to let him know how much I loved him.

My parents were much more strict about when and who my sister dated. It was as if they had all their hopes set on her, while I was the 'black sheep', not likely to turn out so they didn't monitor me as closely.

But this was only the beginning of the story. This was the first of only two times in my life that I felt the deep rush of oxytocin. The reason oxytocin is so strong and defies logic is that otherwise we wouldn't agree to what the relationship is meant to teach us. And if there's any positive feelings left when it fades, there is the potential for true love.

The reverse exchange came next where our Quebec billots came to stay at our homes. One of the two exciting events was a trip to Niagara Falls. I remember intentionally missing the bus back with another girl from Unionville, and the bus left without us. We hitchhiked home. The other event was a fancy dinner at the Royal York. I remember that as a very happy evening, confirmed by a photo.

Rebellion

My cousin Jurek married his girlfriend Dorothy. She had a beautiful wedding dress with a hundred buttons from the neck down her back. Their wedding reception was my life changing introduction to alcohol. Because my parents allowed us to drink things like sherry, brandy and alcoholic eggnog on special occasions, it's not like I had a burning curiosity. But Toronto Maple Leafs player Mike Pelyk, a friend of the groom, was tending the open bar and decided to have some fun with me. As this was my first introduction to cocktails, he suggested different drinks for me to try. No one kept an eye on me. I don't remember how many I had, but I'll never forget that the last one was a rum and coke, as I spent the rest of the night with my head spinning while puking my guts out into the toilet. Where that was, or how I got home, I don't remember. I also don't remember my parents being in the least concerned. To this day, even the thought of it has brought that memory back to me with a very negative reaction. I know that that experience has kept me from drinking to excess.

I had been keeping in touch with Jimmy Morningstar as well as my friends from Roncesvalles and on the Victoria Day long weekend Bogdan, his sister, her boyfriend and I made the plan to travel to Northern Ontario to attend a dance. Since no one had access to a vehicle, we decided to hitchhike. As I was going to be gone overnight, I informed my parents of my plans.

Predictably they were outraged and forbade it. My father announced to me that the locks would be changed when I returned and I would be disowned. In other words, I would no longer be their daughter. I was more of a rebel than Basia. Her life was so predictable and boring and good: school, homework, orchestra practice and several after school jobs. I saw that her way didn't get approval, so I wanted to see if they cared if I was a little wild. They showed no concern, only anger.

By this time I'd also had two years of being under Michael's steadily increasing influence not to require my parents' approval, permission, advice, compliments or encouragement. By his consistent rejection and disdain, my father had inadvertently taught me to seek it from others who gave it freely.

And so I shrugged my shoulders, packed a backpack and set out on an adventure. The four of us had no trouble catching rides all the way up to Sudbury. By the time we got there, it was late afternoon. I called Jimmy to let him know we were on our way and that we'd meet him at the hall in Blind River where his band was scheduled to play. At this point it was getting difficult to catch a ride, so we adopted a common though devious plan: the two girls would stick our thumbs out, while the guys would hide in the ditch.

This method worked quickly but the first car that stopped was a red convertible sports car with a very small back seat and so we declined. The second car to stop was a full size sedan and the fellow driving didn't mind our ruse. We soon found out why: he was noticeably over the limit, but thanks to his knowledge of the territory, got us safely to Blind River.

We enjoyed the dance, and forging new friendships. It was now close to midnight and since Jimmy had nowhere to house the four of us, we ended up spending the night at the drive-in. Crammed in his friend's spacious convertible we watched an all night marathon of movies that lasted till dawn when the rising sun and birds flying in front of the screen added hilarity to our 'lack-of-sleep' hallucinations. Memorable.

And so was the lecture I received upon my return. No, the police had not been called, the locks had not been changed, the door was not even bolted. All that happened was that I was advised by my father that he decided that he hadn't been strict enough with me and he would now change his way of parenting. He informed me that it was obvious to him that he hadn't said 'no' to me enough. So from now on, his answer 'no' would be at least twice as frequent arbitrarily as his 'yes'. Obedience was high on my father's list.

It took me less than five minutes to figure this out to my advantage: whenever I wanted a 'yes' answer, all I had to do was to use up the 'no' answers on things I didn't care about. This was a major turning point and I lost any remaining respect that I had for this man.

At the age of almost seventeen, I swore that if I was lucky enough to have any, I would never do that to my children.

My sister, now 20 years old, had graduated from Bloor C.I. and got a job as a teller at a bank down on Queen St. She had been dating Stefan for about a year and all was well, until one day our father got upset to see her sitting on her boyfriend's lap on the balcony. Not being one to deal with issues himself, he instructed our mother. She told her never to see Stefan again. This was only the second boyfriend that she had brought home in a period of five years and my sister, not having forgiven her for forbidding the relationship with Jim Williams, decided she had enough of the authoritarian dictatorship and was moving out.

When we left Poland, most of our baggage was my father's library. This man read any and all books on psychology that he could get his hands on. Which was ironic as he hated his older brother who became a psychiatrist and his biggest complaint against the world was that everyone was trying to brainwash everyone else. Funny; the only person that I had in my life that I saw intent on brainwashing all those around him, was my father.

He never changed to the end of his life: continued to force his dogma on others at every opportunity. Spewing constant negative one liners.

If we ever looked dubious or dared to disagree, he would remind us that he is only telling us the truth for our own good, and if we had an aversion to his truth then we were naive. He called it self importance and told us that "everyone wanted to be important" (this was said with a certain pose) yet how stupid that goal was: "we were insignificant like ants, and better off dead". In the same way he justified his criticisms and put downs: "This is a free world and I have the right to speak my opinion." Unfortunately to me, it was like being fed arsenic with every meal. I would literally feel sick to my stomach.

"And the day came when the pain it took to hang on, was far greater than the pain it took to let go."

We also had enough of the harsh way he treated our mother. By this time she was docile, frightened, without a mind of her own, just trying to balance supporting her daughters with doing whatever it took to keep her husband from committing her to a psychiatric institution. Though she made the money, he controlled the bank account and the spending. She had no idea that she had any rights at all if she decided to leave him.

Our parents fighting became more frequent and since it was always about us, I believed that they would be happier when the sources of their disagreements were no longer on site. Since my father's favorite topic for browbeating and berating my mother was us, I thought removing myself as well, would be the kindest thing I could do for her. I thought if he was no longer irritated by me, he would stop picking on her. They would have the opportunity to actually get along and save their marriage once we were out of the picture. What I didn't realize was that we left the weakest one behind with the wolf. He loved nothing better than to torment people with mind games and now he was no longer outnumbered.

But there was also a deep, as yet unrecognized scream for survival and finally I'd also had enough and decided to move out with my sister. Even though we didn't get along, I also missed my old neighbourhood and school, so I wasn't going to let her leave without me. My mother never forgave us for leaving her behind.

I still had my job at a Hilton Stauffer Reducing Salon and requested a transfer to a downtown location while my sister continued on at the bank. Stefan found a cozy, little one bedroom walkup at 66-B Parkway Ave. in the Roncesvalles district of Toronto for us. The location was great because it was halfway between my old highschool Bloor C.I. and her bank. This time I didn't mind the long walk to and from school.

The first thing we did was get some paint. The landlord told us we could choose any colour we wanted, took us to the paint store and paid for the paint. I remember being amazed at not being told what to buy. Being the early '70's, the kitchen became orange, to go with the brown cupboards. Three walls of the bedroom got a coat of light blue, while the ceiling and remaining wall became violet. We painted the bathroom pink and violet since we had a bit of that color left. The little living room got a coat of burgundy with black doors, ceiling, trim and shelving. We got high on the paint fumes and laughed as we painted. Dad gave us a mahogany shelf and we painted that too. He was horrified how we abused such expensive wood and took it back. I remember buying black shelf brackets, supports and matching shelves for the living room. I also splurged and got a Panasonic AM/FM cassette player with the ability to record. What a joy it was to be able to record songs from CHUM radio station!

Our landlord was very accommodating and it was a great feeling to do as we chose. The second thing we did was get a beautiful little orange kitten.

I now changed the spelling of my name to Renny. I was happy to be back at Bloor C.I. for grade 12 though having missed almost two years there, I now felt out of place. My course load was easy. The rules had changed and the standards had been lowered significantly. No more compulsory subjects: all classes were now optional. I took English, French, Grade 11 and 12 Russian, Math and P.E. I was disappointed that Bloor didn't offer Computer Science as I had really enjoyed it in my other high school. I joined an after school yoga class, held on the auditorium stage.

What was the unexpected complication was my uncompromising honesty.

When I had a dentist or doctor appointment, I would write myself a note and sign it. This apparently was not okay. I was summoned to the vice principal's office to explain. Since I was not living with my parents, who should sign? My parents should, I was told. Between school and my job, I was not willing to spend two hours on the bus to accomplish that. So I asked if he would prefer that I forge their signature? That was definitely not okay, though it was a well known but ignored fact that many kids did it. I had principles and was not willing to do the easy thing. I was seventeen and proud of my semi independence. Even my sister was not my guardian. But the rules were the rules and though my argument was honorable, reasonable and logical, the vice principal had no choice but to follow the rules and I was given a detention: which meant that I had to come to school two hours early and sit in the cafeteria with the other delinquents. No problem, I saved up my homework and studied during that time.

This process transpired approximately once a month during the course of the year, and by the third or fourth time, I merely had to poke my smiling head in and exchange slips of paper with the sighing vice principal.

I was also back in music and did the Royal Conservatory voice program that I graduated with a score of 74%. This increased my confidence and I entered several talent contests, but did not do well. I remember that one contest in particular required the song "Both Sides Now" and just didn't have the range or confidence on such a difficult piece. I got good marks on my two choices, but of course it's much easier to remember the criticism rather than praise, so I don't remember what those two songs were.

I joined the Bloor Cycle Club and bought a gray Bottecchia racing bike. My pride and joy. Andrew Kent was the owner's son and his birthday was June 1st like mine.

It was mostly a happy time with freedom to finally have friends over, though Lloyd, Peter and Sue from my previous school rarely dropped by as it was quite a distance from Willowdale. Scott came around every so often as well. I remember going to a Crosby Stills, Nash and Young concert at Varsity Arena on September 28th, but not with who. The ticket was $7.

Another time Basia had $5 left until the next payday and I had some subway tokens and free tickets for a Balalaika concert downtown. We went to a fancy restaurant for coffee after.

She was blond and flirtatious, well acquainted with makeup and heels. My hair was mousy brown and I was painfully shy. I rebelliously resisted makeup and still wore kneesocks. This did not work well as a dating strategy especially when one of the most popular slogans at this time was a Clairol hair dye commercial that 'blondes have more fun'.

Unfortunately my mother told me if I used it my hair would fall out. So my conclusion was that my sister was blessed and I was cursed.

Where she was coy, I was too honest. I refused to play any dating games and couldn't understand why boys were happy to have me for a friend but didn't chase me. Wearing knee sox would naturally put you in the friend zone. I remember Jurek setting me up on a date with a boy named Graham. It was exciting to go on a date without parental disapproval. But the joy was short lived as the second time that he came by, it was to pick up my sister. I remember her attitude was "all is fair in love and war".

We fought a lot and sometimes went for days without speaking to each other. As when we were children in Poland, to her, our relationship was always one of competition whereas I was seeking an alliance.

Chapter 13 - 1972

My heartthrob was still Scott. Approximately every month and a half, he would show up and sweep me off my feet again... Amazingly he did not fall under my sister's spell and only had eyes for me. When he was around me that is. When he wasn't, he was once again seeing his on and off ex-girlfriend, which I wasn't aware of at this time. He continued to teach me to hold eye contact and to kiss, but refused to allow it to go any further. Yet he continued to fill my ears with sweet nothings.

I remember he took me to London, (Ontario) to meet his friend Tom and his wife and kids. He also took me to meet his parents Alex and Geraldine multiple times. They had both served during WW2 and being British, they were not happy about the potential German daughter-in-law. While I, being Polish, was a much more pleasant prospect. They were so eager to accept me.

Then one night Scott called me and told me that he was so conflicted in his feelings. He was unhappy with his girlfriend and didn't know how to get out of the commitment he made to marry her by taking her virginity so he overdosed on sleeping pills and my voice was the last thing that he wanted to hear.

I knew I had to keep him awake, and I knew I should call an ambulance. But he wouldn't let me hang up and I had no way to make another call at the same time. I was able to keep him talking till dawn, so he obviously didn't take enough. He said he'd see me soon and then I didn't hear from him for another several weeks.

I continued to hang out at MacGregor park on St. Helen's Ave. with Dea's friends, Jack McEwan, Butch, Andrew and Dave. My friend Susan who was now dating Andrew, often came down to join us. One of my highlight memories was seeing Scott's Camaro stop by the park. He leaned on it and watched me as I ran to him. Without a glance back, I was in his car and in heaven again.

I don't remember where we'd go or what we'd do, but the feeling of bliss I felt on those occasions is unforgettable. But those times were few and far between. He had told me in the past that he was not interested in taking my virginity. He was still too much of a gentleman to do so. Instead, he made love to me with his words.

In the meantime I hung out with Dea's friends who were the only highschool kids willing to let me be part of their group. I was taken along to parties where they all smoked marijuana but allowed me to be who I was: not interested. I did try mj. once out of curiosity. Since I had never learned to inhale, Butch blew it into my mouth. I spent the rest of the evening watching a grandfather clock pendulum swing side to side. They couldn't get me to say anything worse than darn. Afterwards I was always either taken home or put in a cab. They protected me and sometimes teased me about how naive and innocent I was. We often frequented a coffee shop near the highschool where we sat late into the night drinking coffee mixed with hot chocolate.

In March of that year, my sister decided to quit her job and head for California. It was a miserable winter as usual. And then on the news, we saw Vancouver with trees in bloom and people playing golf and sailing. That image did it for her and she gave her notice the next day. Stefan was still determined to persuade her to marry him. She responded that she was taking off on a holiday and would give him an answer if and when she returned. Within two weeks, she was gone. I had no way of making the next month's rent on my own, so I gave away much including the black shelving that we had. Scott loved it all so I gave it to him when I moved.

I moved to an upstairs rented room in a house at 70 Emerson Street, finally a glorious five minute walk to school! A family lived there whose daughter was an airline stewardess. There were a couple more renters and we shared the kitchen and bathroom. I quickly wore out my welcome when, having acquired a sense of independence, I made arrangements for my own phone line to be installed in my room, without first discussing it with the owners. There was no cost to them, so no reason for them to complain, but they got upset when the phone tech was running new wires into the house. Another lesson learned.

School counselling put me in touch with IODE (*The Imperial Order Daughters of the Empire (IODE) is a women's charitable organization based in Canada. It provides scholarships, bursaries, book prizes, and awards, and pursues other philanthropic and educational projects in various communities across Canada.*) and along with a small donation from them, I added a Saturday shift in the gift shop of St. Joseph's Hospital. This got me through till the end of the school year.

By May I had enough of the teasing from my girlfriends. From the teasing, I deducted that I was treated as a child, since I was still a virgin. Somehow that had turned into an unwelcome problem that needed a solution. Somehow it appeared to stand in the way of having a boyfriend! Even with my sister's absence and hence no competition or comparisons, I felt that there was something very wrong with me to make me so undesirable. Dea had a steady boyfriend and so did Susan who was dating Andy, and so did Jack whom I greatly admired and had a secret crush on. I liked Andy's brother Danny but he wasn't at all interested.

Jack had been in a long term on and off relationship with Jessica and I hadn't even considered having a chance there. One day he approached me at lunchtime and asked if he could talk to me in private. I remember he took me to a nearby building. He asked me what my plans were after highschool. Trying so hard to show that I was independent, I told him I'd like to be a stewardess and travel. Had I asked him why, I likely would have given a very different answer. He then said that he had a very good job lined up with the city parks department and was ready to get married and start a family. He had three prospects that he was considering and I had just been eliminated! The funny thing is that he hadn't even taken me out on a date, yet I was crushed. The truth was that I hated the whole feminist movement and more than anything, wanted to be a wife and mother. But it was too late.

I was almost 18 and the only one that hadn't had sex. I heard everywhere that it was the responsible thing to do and so I got a prescription for birth control pills from the doctor whose children my sister used to babysit. There were no abstinence messages in the early '70's. The moral values of the 50's and early 60's had all but disappeared. The current message was loud and clear: free love, have fun, just be responsible.

I went to see Scott at his Albany Ave. address where he had a room upstairs. I had been there before, but this time I came unexpectedly. He was lying on his bed and regrettably, I had no idea what to do or say! I remember the layout of this room to this day. I remember the small table with carvings on it that matched his arm tattoos with the word "Barb". He said he regretted them. I remember it being awkward and he finally got up and we went for a walk.

I asked Michael for advice and he strongly discouraged me from pursuing Scott. He wasn't worthy and would just use me. I could do so much better. He offered to initiate me himself based on his vast experience as a lover of women, but I wasn't buying it.

Butch told me that there was a mid 30's woman in the neighbourhood who took it upon herself to initiate teen boys by encouraging them to 'get it over with' and with their first experience out of the way, they didn't feel the need to bother girls and could court them properly. This was the early '70's, the time of free love, and there were no virgins, boys or girls, over the age of 16 except for me. I asked him if he would help me to 'get it over with' and after a couple of weeks, he finally agreed. A few days after my 18th birthday, he came over to my rented room, we did the bare minimum and it was done. I was now a woman.

Odds are your first sexual experience wasn't what you thought it would be. Who knew what to expect -- and what you'd be thinking afterward? I still didn't have the foggiest notion of what sex was about. That initiation was a letdown, painful for the flesh but even more so for the psyche. The next few days were consumed in reflection that was jumbled and repetitive and led to no conclusion. Again and again, I would wonder whether this deeply unsatisfying event was what made the entire world revolve on its axis? I can remember thinking that this is one rite of passage I could have easily left out. We parted on amicable terms, but not without a large helping of disappointment. Even though there was shared affection in that room where I was surrendering my innocence, I felt regretful and penitent -- nowhere near the joyous woman of experience I was now supposed to be. Silly goose that I was, I felt forever changed -- and not in a good way.

I was now ready but Scott was nowhere around. It seemed that life had other plans. Other issues developed that turned out to be more advanced lessons.

"Guard your heart more than anything else, because the source of your life flows from it"
- Proverbs 4:23

My parents had moved from our 3 bedroom Parkway Forest Dr. apartment to a one bedroom in the heart of Don Mills. I was sitting on the bus on my way there one day, when I noticed a good looking dark haired boy glancing at me. He was standing nearby and smiled each time I looked his way. He kept looking at me, trying to catch my eye and I thought since there's no way a guy that good looking would ever be interested in a relationship with me, why not have a little fun. I was enjoying myself pretending to be someone else. I got off on my stop and noticed that so did he. He had actually missed his stop a few miles back. Rather than suffer the inevitable rejection when he heard my accent, I claimed to be a French exchange student. When he spoke to me, I decided to continue my fantasy and responded with a mixture of French and English with a convincing French accent. I really did not think I would ever see him again. Great looking guys like him rarely continued their interest in a wallflower such as I. He was intrigued so much that he invited me for coffee. We had a wonderful chat and he promised to call me.

And call me he did. I continued the charade not imagining that I would ever see him again, but obviously being someone I wasn't, was a lot more appealing to boys. He probed me with questions and several days later, he showed up at my school. I now had to come clean about my deception. He was angry and that was the first red flag. His reaction also cautioned me about disclosing my lack of virginity. He'd had one girlfriend before me who broke his heart and he found it hard to trust and needed to be in control of the relationship.

Chris had an after school job at a beautiful counter restaurant called Diana Sweets at 187 Yonge St. On the nights he worked, I'd go downtown to meet him and he'd serve me an amazing dessert. He always wore beautiful tapered button down shirts and sometimes we stopped to buy him a new shirt. He also taught me how to cook a steak properly. He was my Adonis, my David and I didn't mind becoming his possession.

I had quit my job at the downtown reducing salon just before I met Chris. The janitor had quit and another girl and I were told that we now had to do the vacuuming, cleaning and disinfecting. Not knowing how to express my point of view, I simply quit on the spot.

My grandmother wanted me to go to Poland with her but the opposition was strong from my parents. In August they had both renounced their Polish citizenship. Being 18, I was left to make my own decision. Having received the very desirable Canadian citizenship just two years prior, they advised me that I would be crazy to return and risk arrest there. Chris said that he would break up with me if I did. Another red flag. Looking back, that was a huge regret as up to meeting him, I wanted nothing more than to return. And how did I then decide to head to B.C. for a week to visit my sister and he was okay with it? I think I took the train to Sicamous and then a bus but all I remember from that time is the winding, rough road with steep terrain and the most beautiful scenery I had ever seen. I fell in love with the orchard that my sister lived on and could talk of nothing else on my return.

Chris had told me that living on my own would be a serious issue for his conservative Greek parents so I talked with my aunt Lidia and she invited me to live with her. This way I became more respectable and he would be able to introduce me. I still had my Saturday job at St. Joseph's and Chris started to pick me up there. One day I got a call that a carton of cigarettes was missing and my boyfriend and I were the likely culprits. Nothing could have been further from the truth as neither of us smoked, but since I was going to move to Don Mills, I wasn't interested in making the effort to clear my name. I told them I was innocent and quit on the spot.

Living with Lidia was a pleasure as well as a challenge. My aunt worked as an accountant at the Ontario Provincial Police office downtown and often came home with a migraine. That meant complete silence as she isolated in her upstairs bedroom. I visited her at work a few times and noticed that the whole large room was a thick fog of cigarette smoke.

When she didn't have a migraine, she wanted to chat. A lot. She was very generous and tuned in to my interests. She shared her love of romance novels with me as well as introducing me to meditation and reincarnation. She bought me the Jane Roberts book "The Education of Oversoul 7" and I was hooked.

Dreams have always been my favorite spiritual gifts to receive. Ever since I escaped into them to return to my homeland, I have sought refuge and guidance in dreams.

Oversoul 7 reinforced that. It also taught me that a strong moral code to Oversouls, is like $$ to mortals. Doing what is right is noticed, recognized and recorded. Doing the right thing under difficult and/or unpleasant circumstances is given special consideration. Doing the right thing when the cost is high, is 'rewarded' with a 'miracle'. And a miracle is when the Divine Force suspends natural law for you.

Living with aunt Lidia I learned even more about the roles of women in my family. She was a classic beauty, dressed impeccably, hardworking, independent and outspoken. But apart from my grandmother who lived with her, she was alone.

More than anything, she wanted a man to share her life with, but it just wasn't to be.

Babusia ate like a bird and she told me it was because if she ate more she wouldn't be able to fit the closet full of brightly colored clothes that Lidia bought her and that would be so wasteful. By now, she had also surrendered to Lidia's pressure and cut, colored and permed her hair in order to be a 'modern' woman. By doing that, she no longer seemed wise. She was also very lonely, but sacrificed her happiness for pleasing her daughter. Her grasp of english was poor and living in the suburbs she was completely dependent on Lidia.

Though Lidia craved a man's love and read voraciously about it, she didn't have it. She confided in me that her ex husband frequently made fun of her bony knees and eventually left her. I don't think she ever got over that. She was an extrovert and fiercely loyal. Her aging german shepherd Kazan was her constant companion.

That summer was wonderful: Chris and I went horseback riding and I taught him to play guitar. One weekend we hitchhiked up to Callander in central Ontario, which is located at the southeast end of Lake Nipissing. We rented a cabin and had a wonderful time. My very first time on water skis was here, getting up on the first try from a sitting position on the dock. What a boost to my confidence! The man with the boat knew how to introduce beginners to the sport and I fell in love with it.

We went on many bike rides together though they weren't very enjoyable for me as I couldn't keep up with him and he would get angry. Once I fell so far behind that I stopped and hid. When he finally back tracked, he got very angry. One time we went horseback riding on the outskirts of Toronto, past Steele Ave. and had a long way back walking in angry silence to find a bus that would allow us to take our bikes home.

Chris now insisted that I move back in with my parents before he could introduce me to his. By the time September came, my parents had bought a condo in downtown Toronto at 40 Homewood Ave. Not wanting to change schools yet again, I decided to attend Bloor C.I. for grade 13 and be a respectable girlfriend to Chris. Besides French, English and Music, I took Ancient Greek. My parents agreed to let me live with them. I got a part time job at a nearby hotel coffee shop and signed up for Grade 13 Russian evening class at nearby Jarvis Collegiate.

My parents, even with their daughters out of the way, had continued to live together, but in an uncomfortable truce. They appeared to be happier when I asked if I could move back in with them, and looked forward to seeing their prodigal daughter safely back home. My father couldn't wait to be proven right.

Looking back, at this crossroad, I wonder if I made a good decision considering all the other factors?

I remember Lidia being very disappointed. She bought me my first cassette: Poppy Family: my favourite singer. She loved me as her niece and really enjoyed sharing girl stuff. I don't doubt that she would have seen and cautioned me about the pitfall that was to come but I didn't have any concerns to share back then. I didn't see the 'red flags'.

I attended Chris' rugby games in the fall and hockey games in the winter. He gave me his jersey which I still have. Many a game I sat on the sidelines and watched him play. He was very good but not popular with the other players. He took me to Maple Leaf games at Maple Leaf Gardens arena downtown. He gave me his Maple Leaf jersey which I've lost. Again he was very good but had no friendships there. He took skating lessons from a dubious, likely gay teacher.

He bought me a gold locket with my initials for Christmas. Michael continued to give me advice and I remember having a graph posted on my wall, encouraging me to reduce the highs and lows of my emotions. The other advice from him was a Socrates quote: "Everything in moderation, including moderation" which took me many years to understand. Scott continued to occasionally call which kept reigniting my confused passions.

The pictures I have from that time only show me with my mother. She and I received matching bathrobes for Christmas. I ended my job at the hotel coffee shop when the cashier demanded $20 from me to cover the check that was absconded on. Since she was sitting by the door, and I ran off my feet, I declined and quit. I was getting tired of all the holiday shifts and hated the uniform which required pantyhose. I never hesitated to quit a job and find another: that was one area where my confidence was strong.

Plus Chris had plans for us for New Year's Eve downtown and that was the first time I would enjoy celebrating it like most people my age. What I remember most was how uncomfortable I was with the room full of strangers and the noise and crowd. Even the kiss at midnight.

Chapter 14 - 1973

Basia wrote to me that she had married Lee in December and that he was the manager of Mr. Sworder's 50 acre orchard on Fleet Road, halfway between Penticton and the village of Naramata. I knew that she disliked Toronto but she never wanted to be a 'farm wife': she was always drawn to the finer things in life. It went against everything I knew about her. Yet since she stayed with Lee since her arrival in the spring of 1972, and then married him, I reasoned that for her to make such a huge change in her outlook, life there must be pretty wonderful.

My sister and her new husband arrived in January on their way to Greece for a holiday. They stayed at 17 Indian Road Crescent, a house my father had bought with the intention of eventually moving there. Basia and Lee met Chris when I organized a party for her wedding celebration.

Chris and I had good times and we made plans for the future. We performed on talent night at Bloor C.I. He played guitar and I played flute which I had started to learn on my own. We sang "If I had a Hammer". I loved Rita Coolridge and Kris Kristopherson duets and we harmonized on one of their songs as well. He took me to eat at a Greek restaurant on College Street at Yonge. I remember it was upstairs and you walked by the open kitchen and chose your food from the buffet there. I remember being impressed at his fluent Greek as he conversed with the staff that obviously knew him - and his food choices for me were delicious.

We took lots of pictures and built a beautiful album which he insisted on keeping at his place. We chose names for the first two of our four future children. His parents still did not approve of me as I wasn't Greek. I even took Ancient Greek in the first semester of Grade 13, but to no avail.

Basia and Lee were back in Penticton and we pored over her letters and decided that we would move out west. We got that idea from watching the movie "Friends" which had come out in 1971. This movie has amazing Elton John songs. So it seemed

most romantic to just plan to run away like Paul and
Michelle in the movie.

"Cast a pebble on the water
Watch the ripples gently spreading
Tiny daughter of the Camargue
We were meant to be together
We were made for one another
In a time it takes to grow up
If only we were old enough
Then they might leave us both alone
So take my hand in your hand
Say it's great to be alive
No one's going to find us
No matter how they try
No one's going to find us
It's wonderful so wild beneath the sky
Sleeping in the open
See the shadows softly moving
Take a train towards the southlands
Our time was never better
We shall pass the sights of splendor
On the door of a new life
It had to happen soon I guess
Whether it is wrong or it is right"

Chris lived with his parents who both worked in restaurants downtown usually from afternoon till late evening. He would pick me up after school and on days when he wasn't working, we would go up to his place in Don Mills. I loved the feeling of finally having a boyfriend and looked forward to seeing him waiting for me by my locker. I was finally wanted and worthy of being loved!

I noticed the fist holes in the walls of his home and ignored them. Chris explained that his parents' arguments sometimes got out of control and restricted me to his room. If I stepped a foot into the kitchen or bathroom, he was obsessive about checking every area for stray hair. He did not want his parents to know that he was bringing a girl home.

One time we heard the door open as his mother arrived unexpectedly early. There was no way to sneak me out and the only time that I met her was as I was being quickly herded from his bedroom to the entry door. She glowered at us and said nothing. On the other hand, my mother felt that as long as I was in by ten p.m, I wasn't having sex.

On other days, we would install door viewers. Michael had procured a great job for us, going into apartment buildings and selling them door to door for $10. All we needed for the job was a hand drill and a box of viewers. Chris drilled the wooden doors, while I measured, marked and installed. We made $5 profit on each one. Minimum wage was around $2 per hour, so we were making at least that.

Then Chris would take me home to my parents' place and we'd squabble and fight about all the things I did wrong. I was grilled about classmates and forbidden to continue friendships with anyone, male or female. Little by little he demanded more and more control over me. These sessions often ended up in the stairway, late at night where I was regularly getting slapped across the face on a regular basis for not giving him the right answers. My parents heard nothing and said nothing. At school my marks dropped from low 70's to low 60's even though I was only taking 3 day classes at Bloor, plus one evening class at Jarvis C.I. Now thinking back on it, this was the moment to leave Chris but why would I when what I had wished for since grade 8, was to have a devoted boyfriend! He was possessive, yes, but didn't that mean that he loved me?

By February of 1973, I could no longer handle both Chris and school. Something in me broke. I knew I had to get free of Chris but didn't know how. Yet he kept insisting that once we were away from Toronto, everything would be so much better and I wanted so badly to believe him.

And out of nowhere, Scott happened to call. He couldn't stop thinking about me. Hearing his soothing voice increased my longing for his kindness and affection. He asked me to go on a work run in Tom Scaiff's 18 wheeler to Chicago. More than anything, I desperately wanted to, as I saw this as not only a chance, however brief, to be with the one that I felt was my true love and treated me kindly but also as a way to get out of the abusive relationship. I was eighteen and confused control with love.

I made the mistake of asking my mother for advice. She strongly advised me not to. Why didn't she believe me about the physical and verbal abuse?? Her reasoning was that if anything happened on this trip, like an accident, she was afraid of what Chris would do if he found out. That was the whole point: I knew that Chris would then be the one to make the choice to break up with me. But wait, then Scott would go back to his commitment and I would be alone again… this was a major crossroads and I was scared to take the wrong road.

It surprises me that as I write this, it still triggers tears.

So I did not go and Chris' demands, two part time jobs and the last year of highschool ended up being just too much pressure. I coped by quitting school without anyone knowing. I still left home at the usual time and I don't remember what I did or where I went, as Chris was still attending his Western Tech High School north of High Park. How he ended up there considering he lived in Don Mills I cannot remember or guess.

I got caught at the end of April. Michael was now married to Wendy and they had set up a private college and somehow he caught on. He was furious, and as my parents' reaction was indifferent, it showed me that he cared. It was unacceptable he said and organized tutors for me to catch me up so that I could graduate grade 13 on time. He said that I must finish what I started. So I caught up 3 months in one. This wasn't a great challenge as I was only taking three subjects: English, French and Music. I had already completed my grade 13 Russian class before Christmas and dropped the Greek class when I realized it was not going to make a difference in how Chris' parents felt about me.

Scott continued to call me every few weeks and it's like I was powerless to resist his loving words. I was worried that I would weaken and agree to meet him and I kept reminding myself that as he was now married, he made his choice and he was off limits. Another reason to move as far away as was possible.

I had to focus on being back at school and having a real boyfriend that I didn't have to share. Having a date, I was really looking forward to attending both our graduations but the teachers went on strike in June and the ceremonies and dinners were postponed till fall by which time we expected to be living in B.C. So no dress, no celebration, not even an acknowledgement from my parents. It was no less than was expected of me so there was nothing to celebrate. My honors diploma was mailed to me.

Short lived paradise

My sister wrote and said that there was work available on the orchard so as Chris' high school finished first, he left for Sworder's orchard in early June. I followed after finishing my exams several weeks later. I knew that I had to put some serious distance between Scott and I and there was no further place to move to than British Columbia. I also switched my birth control to an IUD, as I was worried that with the change in environment I might turn forgetful.

I remember how happy Chris was to see me, with his job in the orchard and with our new life there. We made a little one bedroom picker's cabin into our home. The fifty acres of fruit trees on the cliffs above Okanagan Lake were breathtaking with their beauty. I brought some household things with me and we bought the rest. My favourite picture of a smiling Mexican boy in a straw hat and holding a jug, came with me. The cabin had a wood stove in the kitchen. It was about a 100 feet down from the manager's house where my sister lived with Lee. The transient workers were housed in bunk style cabins closer to the road.

On June 16th, I wrote Livia this letter:

"Dear Livia,

There is so much to tell I hardly know where to start. First, I got on the 9:30 direct flight to Vancouver and I got there at noon. At 2:15, I got on the plane to Penticton and I got in at 3:30. The taxi dropped me off near where Lee was, so I saw him first. Then he said Chris was past the house working, so I saw my sister on the way. When I saw Chris up in a tree on a ladder thinning pears, I came up behind him and whistled. He recognized our special signal but he couldn't see me at first. Anyway, he was really glad to see me. I just sat around till he finished at 5pm.

You should see this place. The house has a large kitchen, the size of yours, there's a wood stove which is really warm, a big cast iron thing. The paint job inside is shitty dark green and gray. The color Chris chose is a dark gold and we've painted the door and one cupboard. I had some money left so I went into town and got some shelf paper and groceries. I painted the wooden table and two chairs yesterday, with the gold paint. For the walls, he's getting some straw yellow paint.

I started getting all the stuff unpacked so it's still a mess. Today I started working on thinning, two hours in the morning and two in the afternoon. I pick my hours and my times when I want to work. There's a lack of help all around here because of the low wages. But we get the house, so it's like we make more. The house has a lot of possibilities, and we're gonna really fix it up nice.

We eat regularly and well. I love cooking (I've also got a Coleman stove) and in the evening we make a fire and cook on that. I bought a set of dishes with a brown, yellow and orange pattern, so now we've got some dishes. We haven't got hot water unless the stove is going. Lee got a car yesterday, so now we don't have to hitch anymore. I'm close enough to my sister but it's far enough too. It's just about 50 yards.

The days are so short and there's so much to do. There's so much room, far from the road and town. You can just walk through the orchard on and on and get sick on cherries. They will be ready to pick in about a week or two. Chris works hard but he looks so healthy and full of energy and warmth. I'll tell you, it didn't take me long to forget Toronto.

I love taking care of everything and fixing this place up. You've got to come after we get settled, if we decide to stay here. Chris loves it as much as I do. We get up at 5:30-6:00 and he leaves at 7am. We get to bed about 10pm. Tonight we're going into town, and if it's not too late, we're going to the pound and get a pup and/or a kitten. There's lots of room and no problem at all.

I wish you could see all this! Last night we went down the cliffs to the lake and I sat on a rock in the water. The beach is short and rocky and the lake's big.

My father bought a house at 17 Indian Rd. Cresc. And he's going to rent it out. He said on

Monday that if you ever need a place, you could rent a room real cheap, because he needs good tenants.

Right now it's lunch time and I'm going to work in about 10 minutes and I have to wash the dishes first.

Take care and write back to us. - Love, Rini"
% J.V. Sworder, RR#1, Naramata Road, Penticton, B.C.

This to me was paradise. The orchard, situated on the edge of Okanagan Lake, had cherry, apricot and peach trees. I arrived just in time for cherry picking. Chris and I painted the inside of the cabin and I helped my sister with her large vegetable garden. I loved walking barefoot, wearing my favourite long dress that I had sewn in Toronto. When we couldn't coordinate with the little microbus, we'd hitchhike into town to do laundry and shopping. In the evenings while the sprinklers came on, we clambered down the path on the steep limestone cliff to the beach below. We got a tan labrador puppy at the pound and named her Brandy. We bought a little car. Life was an amazing dream and for a time, we couldn't be happier. There were no phone calls and no reminders of past friendships.

It was just Chris and I, and that made him very happy. And when he was happy, he treated me well.

One weekend we hitched a ride to Kelowna for a Susan Jacks concert and camped by Knox Mountain. I remember the different glimpse of Okanagan Lake shortly after passing Westbank. This was before all the billboards were put up. It made a very strong impression on me. The surrounding hills were the closest thing to my beloved area around my hometown of Cieszyn and the drive down to the bridge was breathtaking.

On July 6, I wrote again to Livia:

"Dear Livia,

I hope you had a really good trip and enjoyed Italy. How did you get along with your Italian against all those natives? Is it true girls there don't mind being pinched on the street? Is it like you expected? I expect a full report.

Cherries are finished. I don't miss the work but I miss eating them. I turned into a monkey, cause it seemed no matter where I started with a ladder, I always ended up in the top middle of the tree. (Usually stuck). We got paid 7 cents a pound which came out to $1.60 an hour or so. Anyway now we're finishing apricots and that's by the hour.

($2 I think)   The guys pick and the girls sort for the packing and canning houses. It's standing 8 hours on your feet by a bin in hot weather.   Which is great, by the way. (the weather, not the work)

Anyway, it's money and right now we're saving up for a stereo. I guess I wrote about our dog Brandy. Our cat got poisoned and died but we want to get another. After work we go swimming to the beach. Not many people, clean water, close. We got an air mattress, and some masks and snorkels. Brandy comes swimming then she rolls in the sand, then deposits herself on our blanket.

My mother likes it here and it's nice having her for a while. Chris' parents write to him in Greek and I've given up hope that they'll ever understand. I'm not sure if you know Barb's pregnant. She's due at the beginning of February. We don't get along that well. She's the foreman's wife and she let's you know it.

I've canned some cherries, dried cots and plan on canning pears. I learned to make pizza and bread. Once a week we go into town so I try to write before that so I can mail it. It's nice being in town only once in a while. Last weekend we went 40 miles north to Kelowna to see Susan Jacks. There was a fair there, with rides and shows. She was good but

Terry wasn't with them. We stayed at a campsite full of other kids.

On the way back we got a ride with a couple who lived in a truck. They had everything there and saw the country that way. Chris got ideas and now he's working to get a van of his own and furnish it. He thinks to travel for 3-4 months next summer.

The sweatshirts are perfect sizes and exactly what I asked for. Both of our thanks. We wear them all the times it's cool and Chris talked of getting more.

You getting ready for school? When do you start? What will you do till then?

Write! Take care and keep happy, love, Rini"

From paradise to hell

Until the day about six weeks after my arrival, the longest and last of several letters arrived from his mother. It was in Greek.

I had gone into town to do laundry and rather than catching the microbus home as expected, I hitched. As I was walking down the driveway to our cabin, I did not see Chris walking through the orchard to meet the bus. Not being on it, he returned to the cabin very angry. It came out that his mother's four page letter had disturbed him deeply.

He refused to translate it for me. As the evening progressed, he got more and more angry. He started to slap me and progressed to hitting. Then punching. Then beating. This lasted for probably two hours when I was finally able to calm him down and we went to sleep exhausted.

I woke up in severe pain and meekly made his breakfast. The orchard owner Mr. Sworder was taking a group of pickers to a neighbour's orchard for the day. After he left, I inspected my battered and bruised body and face in the mirror. I was in a panic: my body was black and blue. The radio was on and I remember finally allowing myself to cry as Carole King's song "It's Too Late" came on. I remembered that we had a rifle in the cabin and I was scared that Chris would decide to kill me when he got home.

"Stayed in bed all mornin' just to pass the time
There's something wrong here there can be no denying'
One of us is changing' or maybe we've just stopped trying'
And it's too late baby now it's too late
Though we really did try to make it
Something inside has died and I can't hide it and I just can't fake it

Oh, no-no-no-no

It used to be so easy livin' here with you
You were light and breezy and I knew just what to do
Now you look so unhappy and I feel like a fool
And it's too late baby now it's too late
Though we really did try to make it
(we can't make it)
Something inside has died and I can't hide it and I just can't fake it
Oh, no-no "

Funny, as I write this, that's not the part that's triggering tears. It's what happened next.

I put on a long sleeved top and walked up to my sister's house. My mother happened to be visiting from Toronto and I got a very strange reaction to my arrival. They were both mad at me as several days prior, I had used the oven to bake some cookies and didn't share any. They both wondered why I was wearing pants and long sleeves in August. I broke down and through my tears and sobs, told them what had happened the night before. I got no sympathy or assistance. I remember being stunned as my mother brought up my insensitivity as an explanation for deserving the beating. My mother basically said "you've made your bed". My sister did not bother notifying her husband. She has no memory of any of this.

I debated where to hide. I could go to Kelowna where I didn't know anyone, or? I called my friend Livia for advice. She immediately said she was sending me $400 and to return to Toronto. I was traumatized and in shock. I hadn't yet learned to surrender my circumstances to God and trust that my inner guidance would present me with alternate choices. Not being clear headed enough to consider other options, I did as I was told. Looking back, I wish I had gone up to Kelowna, as he would never have thought to look for me there. But I was too traumatized to think clearly. I should never have returned to Toronto, but I did what Livia advised: the only person who offered assistance. If I had my own money, I might have gone to Kelowna, even without knowing anyone there. But because Livia lent me the $$, it felt like I should do what she told me to.

I quickly packed a bag and hitched to Penticton. The money transfer was waiting for me at the bank. The earliest flight out was late afternoon, and I couldn't chance waiting around for the next 4 hours. I was sure Chris would catch up with me and kill me. So I left on the next Greyhound to Calgary where I caught a flight back to Toronto.

It's ironic that as badly as I wanted a boyfriend, none of the boys that I liked throughout highschool, liked me back; while the ones that wanted me, (Lloyd and Peter) I didn't want them. And the only one I loved was Scott who wasn't available. So I settled for Chris and confused abuse with love.

Back to square one

My parents owned a house on Indian Rd. Cresc. at this time, and planned to renovate it and move in. When I went to collect the things I left behind, I learned that everything of mine had been thrown away after I left for B.C. My parents were not sentimental and to leave anything at their place was considered a serious imposition. Among other things, I missed my Scout cross. It wasn't until 2019 that I was able to finally find another one to replace it.

But in the meantime I was able to rent a room and with the help of a white persian cat I bought, I started to heal there. My friend Susan rented the other downstairs room. I remember a trip downtown where we came across The Guess Who playing a concert in a warehouse on the east side of the waterfront but other than that, we no longer had much in common and did not spend time together.

Wanting to avoid more pain and rejection, I was determined to keep Scott from knowing that I had returned.

I contacted Michael who by this time had given up on his private college and his second marriage (she was so heartbroken that she attempted suicide), and he was now into promoting concerts. I remember meeting Canadian singer Bruce Cockburn. He also opened an after hours club called the Banana Factory. He picked me up and I unburdened myself to him. My heart and soul was shattered and he plied me with wine and compassion. Then put me to bed in the upstairs loft where he lived. Having groomed me for 5 years by this time, I was easy prey. In his words he 'made love to me'. In mine, he took unfair advantage when I was at my weakest point.

I needed practical help as well as someone to lean on emotionally because my life fell apart in spite of all the spiritual wisdom that I had subconsciously gained.

For years I had believed him when he talked to me about the value of sexual experiences and how he could teach me what no one else could. I re-evaluated the situation and I now know that I had been groomed for several years prior.

I don't see the point of throwing a bomb into someone's life. I don't want to destroy but an acknowledgement and an apology would be nice.

I'm more sad than angry. Sad for a 14 year-old me. Sad for the adult me that still thought it was a choice I made. Groomers are skilled operators and at 14, 15, 16, I was not aware of the warning signs. If an adult, someone you know is paying too much attention to a teenage girl; sweettalking, kissing, caressing or even trying to have sex with an underage minor, they are committing a crime, even if the minor doesn't know it.

Grooming is real. It wasn't my fault that I was mentally massaged into thinking it's okay. It is not. I know this now. When it happened, I was 19, had recently left an abusive boyfriend and my parents pretty much told me to fend for myself. And in the upstairs loft above the club, the wolf pounced on me at my most vulnerable.

Testing my options

My first attempts at finding a job did not turn out well. I loved horses and when I saw an ad for a live-in position at a quarter horse ranch a substantial distance out of town, I was excited. I took the bus as far as I was able and a pick up truck met me there to take me the rest of the way. I lasted a day and a half. I didn't mind mucking out the stables and I loved taking care of the horses and living in the bunkhouse with the other girls was fine too. Until I asked why the bunkhouse was being referred to as the 'cat' house, since I hadn't spotted any cats yet. Silly and naive me. I packed my bag and after an uneasy sleep, left the next day.

The next job was at a telemarketing office selling magazine subscriptions by phone. We were given several lists of ascending numbers and expected to make high pressure sales calls. The reactions people rightly had to these invasive, unwelcome calls meant that I didn't even make it 'till lunch. My father's words rang in my ears: I was rejected because I was imposing myself. It's like he almost relished seeing my downfall.

My mother was back from my sister's now and I humbled myself enough to ask for her advice. Because I craved my mother's love and attention, I asked her advice not knowing that it's dangerous to follow the advice of someone who not only doesn't like you, but who is not living the kind of life that you seek.

My father told me that they would be prepared to pay for university if I was willing to fulfill his dream and go into either engineering or architecture. Apart from not having any interest in either of those directions, having focused on languages and music in highschool, I was not in any way shape or form prepared. I knew that I had very poor study skills. As long as I paid attention to the teaching done in class, I was capable of excelling. But I knew that university was different in that it was a much more 'on your own' learning environment.

Where others read haltingly, I had been the kid who was plowing two grades ahead in the reading workbooks.

"These are the kids who turned in a completed book report of a novel for their fifth-grade project. It isn't that they never failed, but at a very early age, they didn't have to fail much; their natural talents kept them at the head of the class.

This teaches a very bad, very false lesson: that success in work mostly depends on natural talent. The kids who race ahead in the readers without much supervision get praised for being smart", says Carol Dweck.

"What are they learning? They're learning that being smart is not about overcoming tough challenges. It's about finding work easy. When they get to college or graduate school and it starts being hard, they don't necessarily know how to deal with that."

My best friend Livia had that advantage as learning did not come easy for her. While I could 'rattle' off my homework in 15 minutes on the morning it was due and aced exams with less, she had to study for hours. Thus she developed the discipline and self study skills necessary to succeed at the post secondary level. Not only that, her father was an engineer with the City of Toronto and she did not resist his influence to follow that career path.

But unless I did as I was told, there was no attempt to advise me or help me. I was left to flounder on my own. My parent's behavior reinforced their teaching. They had no concern for my well being because as a person in my own right, I had no value to them.

I had a gift for languages and had my parents given me even a bit of encouragement, I would have been willing to give university a try. Looking back, I could have gone into a career as a translator or possibly something in the diplomatic core. I remember submitting an application to Air Canada and being called in for an interview. I had the desired qualifications for a ground hostess and was asked how I saw my future. I made the mistake of saying that I hoped to live in a small town. That pretty much ended my chance there as that showed that I was not willing to live in Vancouver, Toronto or Montreal. So any post university education would not guarantee me a job in a small town: not languages, not architecture and not engineering. That was the first major and confusing crossroad for both my sister and I: not wanting to live in the big city but while she wanted the amenities that came with big city living, I wanted to use my languages. I don't think we knew that we could not have both: we had to pick one and give up the other.

I was homesick and continued to dream of my hometown Cieszyn. The political situation there was dire; it just didn't make any sense to even consider going for a visit. Not only that, there was a chance that the communist government would not recognize my Canadian citizenship and passport and might not allow me to leave. I was told once again I'd be crazy to risk it.

The place that I fell in love with was Kelowna and I couldn't get it out of my mind. I decided I would move there, and as I still needed a job to earn the needed money, I drifted back to the one person that was ever ready to listen and help. Michael made me a coat check girl at his after hours club and sent me to his ex Alena, who now ran a temp agency. My first placement was at Commercial Union Insurance company on University Ave. where, not having any other useful skills, I did filing for three months. As soon as I could, I returned to Alena and she placed me at Proctor & Gamble's head office on St. Clair Avenue and I was able to pay Livia back the $400 she sent me. I was now the traffic clerk for Western Canada as well as coat check girl on the weekends where I worked from midnight to 5am. A glass of wine was often placed on the counter in front of me and I learned to invoke a zigzag high from it. Closing my eyes and moving them up as well as side to side gave me a feeling of euphoria.

I met many famous people at the Banana Factory, most notably Harry Belafonte who was the most gracious famous person I ever met. On the other end of the spectrum was Michael Parks, the star of the TV series "Then Came Bronson". When he realized that I was a fan, his behaviour turned sleazy. In between, I met many jazz musicians: Moe Koffman, Don Thompson, Guido Basso, Stan Getz and Kathy and Ted Moses. Doug Cole (who died in June 2012) was owner of George's Spaghetti House, which was the first jazz club in Toronto. Michael included me in many dinners there as well as at Bourbon Street.

Livia told me that Chris had arrived 3 weeks after me and kept calling her to find out where I was. He managed to convince her that he was genuinely sorry and wanted to beg my forgiveness and she finally gave him my number. He gave me the same bullshit line and I, under Livia's influence, fell for it as well. One week after he persuaded me to get back together, he dumped me with the parting words that "nobody breaks up with me". What a fool I was and easy prey due to my once again shattered heart. At least I hadn't suffered any beatings during that week but the resentment I felt at her betrayal lasted for many years.

The tracks had been moved one more time for the benefit of my inner growth

Since I proved my judgement to be so deficient, I needed direction and Michael was quick to plan out my life for me. He encouraged me to continue with music, but play the flute rather than guitar or piano. He arranged for Kathy Moses to teach me. This did not last long as my plastic upper teeth could not handle the mouth position necessary. Plus as much as I tried, I just could not fall in love with jazz music. Michael picked out a car for me from his used car salesmen friends Stan and Ivan; a gray liftback Renault with leather seats. I took out my first loan for the $900 payment. Not a car I was proud of driving, but I trusted that he knew best.

I wanted to learn how to dress, how to walk, etc. so I could feel more grown up and without approval, I signed up for a finishing course that cost $1,000. Michael was shocked and forbade it, calling it a scam and a waste of money, when his ex Alena would be able to teach me all that at no cost. For a start, he advised that I cut my long hair into something edgy and modern. He rightfully pointed out that I used my hair to hide behind. I resisted his suggestion of short at the back and longer at the front, but did get it cut by his hairstylist friend Fernando who cut it short and I hated it. And after taking me shopping for makeup and a beige shirt dress that was clingy and not at all my style, Alena was of little help. I didn't realize at the time how much she resented me.

Besides the Banana Factory, Michael was also working at the Datsun dealership and along with the other salesmen, driving the demos home.

On the weekends he allowed me to tag along with the group to Mosport Race Track where we burned rubber on the days that it wasn't in use. He now rented an apartment with one of the mechanics at Mosport named John. Other weekends we raced around on small, rented sailboats on Lake Scugog, out of Port Perry, north of Oshawa.

He attempted to pick out my boyfriends. My heart was craving the confidence and approval that Scott was always so good at providing but I continued to resist getting a message to him. Michael said that with his criminal record, he wasn't good enough for me and I should steer clear of him. But now I was the one who felt unworthy. Little did I know that he was still unable to get me out of his mind.

One day when I walked into the dealership dressed in a mini skirt, turtleneck and tights, I caught the eye of one of the salesmen by the name of Philip. He was tall and handsome, had recently arrived from Portugal, fluent in 6 languages, martial arts and flew helicopters. Michael allowed him to take me out on a date. After an amazing dinner during which we conversed solely in French, he brought me home. I had had an amazing evening to remember and hoped for many more. As I allowed him to kiss me goodnight, he forced his way inside and refused to leave until I put out. I managed to throw him out and cried myself to sleep. Next morning I told Michael about it. What a huge disappointment that was. And awkward on the next group get togethers. His friend Zbycho also asked to take me out, but I wasn't interested. He was the reason for Michael and Alena's marriage breaking up and I didn't want to have anything to do with him. But that didn't stop him from calling me late at night drunk, professing his love.

I attempted to overcome my lack of confidence in many other ways but I couldn't shake the feeling that I just didn't fit in with this group who were all 7-8 years older than me. I remember after one wonderful outing everyone gathered at Michael and John's apartment for a spontaneous dinner. There were six people and me. I remember being very uncomfortable with the odd number and lack of adequate seating. My father's voice echoed loudly in my head that I wasn't actually wanted there and needed to save myself from embarrassment and leave. Objections were lobbied but I didn't believe they were sincere.

Looking back, as an introvert I felt drained by the excitement of the day and my ability to stay engaged ran out. I shocked everyone when I excused myself and left. In my insecure state I somehow reasoned that it would be okay for me to reappear for dessert so I returned a couple of hours later and proved my father's words: I wasn't welcome and it was very awkward and difficult for people to understand my behavior.

I remember cosigning a $2,000 loan for Danusia's sister Barbara who had been studying in England and with Lidia's help, immigrated to Canada.

Doing things alone was much easier than navigating social situations. I signed up for motorcycle lessons and finished the course, but did not have a motorcycle to use for the road test so it didn't get added to my driver's license.

Michael had been teaching at Arthur Murray's and being occasionally between girlfriends, took me dancing. I loved it and had a burning passion to improve. I signed up for ballroom dance lessons at Mo-Mo's Discount Dance Studio at 782 Yonge St. There I met a dancer who invited me to a party that turned out to be at Fernando the hairdresser's place. Having had too much to drink and no way to get home, I, like several other people, fell asleep on the floor. Several hours later I was woken up to an attempt at being gently raped (if that's possible). I was shocked and quickly adjusted my clothing and got out of there. It was 5am as I made my way home full of self hatred as I blamed only myself for being so stupid. Once again, I shared my troubles with Michael, as that just seemed to be the norm in my disappointing life. I was desperate for acceptance and he gave it.

That Christmas, there was the usual family get-together at Lidia's house. Michael showed up alone, as his daughter Michelle was spending the holiday with her mother Alena and her new boyfriend Harvey.

I had arrived with my parents, but as they still lived downtown, Michael offered to drop me off at home. He seemed in an especially happy mood, as if he was hiding a secret. Family members noticed the connection between us but said nothing. I was 19 and he was 26. Once again, no one felt the responsibility to protect me or at least to take me aside and attempt to caution me. When we got into his car and were driving away, he told me that he was kidnapping me for the next few days. Without stopping to even get a toothbrush or a change of clothes, we drove north to a cottage near Bobcaygeon belonging to (I believe) Doug Cole. Wine was on the table and a turkey feast was in the oven after which he seduced me once again and claimed me as his girlfriend.

Though my life was filled with exciting experiences that shaped the character I had chosen to play in this existence, it did not feel like my life.

Chapter 15 - 1974

From the Frying Pan Into the Fire

Having a car and a job I loved, I rented a second floor walkup at 1989-B Yonge Street with 2 girls from work. This was often a challenge as my co-worker Pam had a boyfriend who stayed over too often and they would leave the kitchen a mess for days on end. She was the traffic clerk for Eastern Canada and her desk was right behind mine, which made life quite uncomfortable. Our male boss was young and like with all female office staff at that time, our desks were outside his office. I loved this job and did it well, but Michael was not satisfied. He was exploring different get rich quick ventures and got me involved in selling Chargex cards part time. Don't remember much about it but I hated scam sales and was therefore useless at it.

He now drove a navy blue, tan interior convertible Fiat Spyder and shared an apartment with John who was a Mosport mechanic. I remember they had raised the floor in the dining area so that it had 2 steps to walk up and if the table wasn't in the way, they'd hit their heads on the light fixture. I spent a lot of time there and occasionally babysat his daughter Michelle. One day she wrote on the wall and I was impressed how he dealt with it. He didn't get angry or punish her, he asked his five year old daughter why she wrote there and told her she needed to scrub it off. When she tried and couldn't, she realized how disappointed he was in her and started to cry. That softened his heart and he comforted her.

Michael finally had a chance to show me what it was like to be adored. He took great delight in this, taking me out to jazz clubs and dancing, as well as cooking for me, washing me and making love to me, teaching me to explore my sensations. I felt adored and spoiled. I thought there was no way any other man would ever be able to match this and I was falling in love which turned out to be an unresolvable problem. Up to that point there was nothing about him that I found desirable as a candidate for my future husband but the oxytocin that was flooding my body had other ideas and I surrendered to the feelings. The highlight was on Valentine's day when a long flower box with a dozen roses was delivered to my desk at work. I was the envy of every girl there and that memory still stands out for me as one of the 10 happiest moments of my life. Never again did I receive flowers at work from a boyfriend. I switched to calling him My-key.

How naive of me to think that my troubles were behind me when they were just about to pick up steam!

He continued his grooming to turn me into his idea of a 'perfect' modern woman. He brought books for me to read like "Jonathan Livingston Seagull", and engaged me in long discussions on the value and desirability of an independent woman who does not get attached. The one that sticks in my head most was "Fear of Flying" by Erica Jong. He really believed that he could mold me, seeing himself as a sort of 'Henry Higgins' on "My Fair Lady".

The relationship worked for him as long as I was detached and unemotional. I had nobody to help me clarify what it was that I wanted. Michael wasn't much different from my father in that he only told me what HE wanted me to do with my life. Plus his strong disapproval of my growing feelings for him was becoming apparent and I was constantly encouraged to see the benefits of living a life of pleasure without the burden of deep (in his words -heavy) emotions.

John's girlfriend was moving in so Michael moved into a basement suite in a house on a side street off St. Clair near Spadina. His next door neighbor was a couple from Mexico. I remember the man's name was Manuel and his wife was very beautiful and friendly to me, but they hardly spoke English.

One weekend that I stayed over, he told me he was going out and I couldn't come. When I persisted as to why, he told me he was going to an orgy (which were very popular in the '70's) and that that was not an appropriate place for me. I was so eager to please by this time that I was actually disappointed to miss out on a chance to show him what a modern woman of the swinging 70's I was. But he would not relent. And as I learned a week later at the doctor's office, no good deed goes unpunished. I was given pills to treat gonorrhea. When I brought this up with him, he gave up trying to convince me that I probably picked it up from Chris, having no symptoms of his own. Eventually though, he admitted that he had sex with a Brazilian woman and I had no right to object as he was free to do whatever he wished.

Carrying the deep hurt of not being wanted as a child, I gravitated towards anyone that gave me the slightest bit of approval, encouragement or attention that I was so desperately lacking from my parents. The late 1960's and the early 1970's were a very confusing and dangerous time for me, and I would have fit in better and been much happier had I been born 10-15 years earlier, or just stayed in conservative Poland.

Barely a month later in spite of having an IUD, I was pregnant. This was unacceptable to him and the torment began where I entered a waking nightmare. I refused to have an abortion and he quickly saw a way to force me into one: he told me that if I had the baby, his life would be finished and he would react by kidnapping the infant and disappearing. So "sure, go ahead and have it, but you will never see the baby or me again." Though I was not ready and he was not the right person, more than anything I wanted to be a mom. I saw this as blackmail and it upset me beyond measure. Days later it turned even more threatening how he would kill us all if I even as much as mentioned it to anyone. Whereas if I agreed, he would commit to me long term. When my resolve weakened, he drove me to my gynecologist who made the arrangements. Several days later he then delivered me to the hospital.

I remember it being early morning and I was put on a ward with five other women. As I lay there in frozen panic, first one was wheeled out and then another. The first one came back and the second one was taken and so on. By this time it was late afternoon and I had somehow become invisible. And relieved. With no word from Michael, I called Lloyd, knowing that he would do anything for me without judgement. He immediately arrived to pick me up and spent the next couple of hours trying to convince me that he would be honored to marry me and give this baby a home. I couldn't believe I had such a good man for a friend but it was impossible as no matter how much I wished it, I just wasn't in love with him. My plan was to head to my sisters as soon as I could.

Several days went by before Michael ambushed me after work to check up on me. Once again he was able to pry the truth out of me and intensified his position with guilt and professions of love and marriage. This time he supervised my hospital trip.

I was left alone in my place to recover. My ob/gyn Doctor Martin was of little help besides prescribing painkillers and telling me that IUDs were much more effective after a first pregnancy and fitted me with another one, a Dalkon Shield (which ended up making 200,000 women in the U.S. infertile). I was forgotten, inconsolable and suicidal. Because I was so devastated and emotional, Michael avoided me. One night I overdosed on pain medication but did not have enough left and woke up the next morning. Another night I got in my car and headed east on the 401. I drove at a reckless speed vacillating between feelings. On one hand I hoped to see flashing lights in my rear view mirror so that I would be forced to confess my crime to a police officer, and on the other hand I wanted to end it in a fiery crash. But the highway was empty and I found myself near Cobourg when my energy ran out.

Out of the blue, Scott called again. He was driving the night shift delivering gasoline to Esso gas stations around town. Did I want to tag along? He picked me up around 6pm and I kept him company on his route. I did not harbor any hopes other than to fill my need of being with someone who cared about me.

The extrovert chatterbox that Scott was, I didn't need to do anything except listen. I did not need to share my trauma and was grateful that he still had no designs on me. Due to his belief that he was being honorable, after 3 years we still hadn't slept together. I remember hiding behind the seats whenever he pulled up to a gas station because if anyone saw he had a passenger, he would get fired. It was wonderful. I loved just being with him. At dawn he dropped me off and I was able to sleep.

Years later, I learned that the song that described our relationship to him, was Jackson Browne's 1974 song:

"Looking through some photographs I found inside a drawer
I was taken by a photograph of you
There were one or two I know that you would have liked a little more
But they didn't show your spirit quite as true.

You were turning 'round to see who was behind you
And I took your childish laughter by surprise
And at the moment that my camera happened to find you
There was just a trace of sorrow in your eyes.

Now the things that I remember seem so distant and so small
Though it hasn't really been that long a time
What I was seeing wasn't really happening at all

Although for a while, our path did seem to climb.

But when you see through love's illusions, there lies
the danger
And your perfect lover just looks like a perfect fool
So you go running off in search of a perfect stranger
While the loneliness seems to spring from your life
Like a fountain from a pool.

Fountain of sorrow, fountain of light
You've known that hollow sound of your own steps
in flight
You've had to hide sometimes, but now you're
alright
And it's good to see your smiling face tonight.

Now for you and me it may not be that hard to reach
our dreams
But that magic feeling never seems to last
And while the future's there for anyone to change,
still you know it seems
It would be easier sometimes to change the past.

I'm just one or two years and a couple of changes
behind you
In my lessons at love's pain and heartache school

Where if you feel too free, and you need something
to remind you
There's this loneliness springing up from your life
Like a fountain from a pool.

Fountain of sorrow, fountain of light
You've known that hollow sound of your own steps
in flight
You've had to struggle, you've had to fight
To keep understanding and compassion in sight
You could be laughing at me, you've got the right
But you go on smiling so clear and so bright."

Lloyd was another story. He offered me a weekend escape to his family's cottage and did everything he could to try and convince me to give him a chance.

My need for male validation would not subside. I even resumed contact with Chris and helped him move. He was now learning to sail on a catamaran on Lake Ontario and did some regular catalogue modeling. But again, being the naive, non judgemental person I was, I ended up confiding my secret to him. Never being a fan of Michael's influence on me, he was outraged and told me that he never wanted to see me again.

Among the phrases that I remember from the 70's are "a man without a woman is only half a man, whereas a woman without a man is nothing at all".

"A woman without her man, is nothing.
A woman: without her, man is nothing."

What a huge difference a bit of punctuation makes. In the age of feminism, where were the women encouraging young girls to value themselves enough not to give in to any man that smiled? Why was the message of sex for pleasure the dominant one?? Why weren't we warned about the damage to the heart?

Scott kept calling every 6 weeks or so but I knew he was seeing Barbara as well, so I eventually drifted back into a semi-relationship with Michael trying very hard not to care and not knowing whether I was still hoping that he would come through on his promise. Some days I was happy to be free of him, other days I was weak.

One night his ex Alena was invited to a party at Manuel's next door. She was proud to show off a ring that she had given Michael for his birthday. Other than that, I got a strong feeling of resentment from her. This was another confirmation of the reason why I had so little comprehension and therefore so little trust in friendships with females up to this time, and would continue to distrust women for the same reasons. Like my sister, I just didn't feel that they wished me well. That somehow they saw me as a threat. At the time Michael told me that I had a secret power but refused to tell me what it was.

Years later, in 2003, I managed to finally persuade him to divulge this 'secret' to me. In Florida Michael told me that what attracted him to me was that unlike most women, I had a complete absence of malice. He said he had never encountered that in a female besides me. And that is what drew him so strongly to me. And that was what women resented in me. And this would continue to surprise me for many years, as various women I hoped to be friends with were uncomfortable with their husband's presence around me.

The 'monster' within me would not be discovered and intentionally released until 1999.

Anyway, back to the ring. When I questioned the generous gift from Alena, he justified it as purely friendship. What about our friendship? The next day he presented me with a cheap ring with the number 8 in it, and proceeded to convince me of its significance for those seeking wealth and prosperity. Which was his goal and not mine, but wore it proudly for many years and still have it put away somewhere.

He now part owned an optical lens company called Plastic Plus with his friend Steve Cohen. Soon my cousin Jurek worked there, as well as Danusia's sister.

My father, unable to find a job at 52, was reduced to accepting a pity offer from Michael. Seeing Michael succeed at everything he failed, he was quietly and irreversibly enraged: he now hated what his Canadian dream life had become even more. He was slow and made many mistakes yet Michael kept him on, adding to my father's humiliation. I was still happy at Procter & Gamble and resisted offers of a job there. But I often stopped by to visit.

That summer, Michael invited me on a road trip to Cape Cod. The trust that he was attempting to rebuild was increased when on the way there, he put the convertible Spyder on auto and suggested I take over driving. I loved this car even more when driving it. It was exhilarating to switch seats at the speed of 50 miles an hour. We booked into a motel and had dinner. The next day Michael rented a sailboat and refused to allow me to put on a lifejacket. I dug my heels in and would not step on board. The more he insisted and insulted me, the more I stuck to my resolve. I was fine with road and air speed but water freaked me out. He could not understand that and since I could not find my voice to explain it, the weekend was ruined. Everything had to be his way as only he knew what was best for me. We checked out and drove the 9 and a half hours back to Toronto in silence. And that was the end of the relationship.

At my job at P&G I met a hobby photographer who asked me if I had done any modelling work (I felt I had, having that one photoshoot three years earlier) and convinced me that I had potential. Not live, as at 5'4" I was too short, but in catalogues. Since both of my roommate co-workers knew him, I had no hesitation in inviting him to do a tasteful lingerie photo shoot of me at my place. Apart from feeling foolish for thinking that I might actually have some desirable, marketable quality, nothing of course materialized from it. Though it made me feel beautiful for a fleeting few moments, it was a quick trip from improved self esteem to confirming my deeply held beliefs that I just wasn't good enough.

In August Scott called to tell me that he could see no way out but to marry his girlfriend. My heart was broken. I asked when and where as I had the crazy fleeing idea of showing up at the church and being the one to object when the minister asked if anyone does. Years later, he confided to me:

"Leading up to that marriage, I was having a very difficult time because of my involvement with you, and my feelings about you, thinking about if I should be doing what I was doing. This was some turmoil for me for a while and I probably did what I did, mostly based on the fact I had built a history and I thought do you know at this stage of the game you have this imbalance you have these two women in front of you and... you have to go this way at this time because if you have any integrity whatsoever this is now the time you have to exercise it.

So that's where my mind was prior to getting married."

I had no idea he was that conflicted while I had no voice: I didn't know how to speak up.

Career switch

Though I really enjoyed my job, Michael finally convinced me to quit Procter & Gamble and got me a job at United Optical which was located at 102 Bloor Street West, where I quickly proved myself a trustworthy and reliable employee. My job started with dusting shelves and progressed to marking lenses, tinting, hardening and hand edging. I was a fast learner and within three months, I was promoted to manager and left in charge. I filled prescriptions, advised customers on frame choices and did the bookkeeping. Michael said I was a natural and encouraged me to get certified as an optician and a tech. I did as I was told and started the Opthalmic Dispensing Course at Ryerson Polytechnical Institute downtown. He also encouraged me to take the course to become contact lens certified but I resisted. I just couldn't imagine teaching people how to put things in their eyes. On my lunch hour, I would check out the Yorkville, Cumberland and Bloor shops around me. It was there that I found my favorite 12 link puzzle ring. It cost me $1 and though, broken, is still my favorite piece of jewelry. Another item was a puzzle of a cartoon train wreck that I held onto for a long time.

The work was easy but lonely. The more competence I showed, the more I was left on my own. Pretty soon Mrs. Tiwana, the wife and co-owner of the store stopped coming in at all. Since my relationship with my two roommates was far from good, I made the decision to move back to the house on Indian Rd. Cres. that my parents still owned and rented out rooms there. I took the subway or rode my bike to work and when I was early, I'd stop at the YM-YWHA on the way, for a game of racquetball. Michael played squash there but that was too rough for me.

Occasionally he still took me out to eat, though. I remember several evenings standing at a designated corner after work, waiting for him to pick me up. It took me a long time to catch on that he was always late. Sometimes it was cold, other times it was raining. Parking downtown was a problem so I usually took the subway to work. The worst waits were over an hour, and when he finally arrived it would be with an excuse claiming some unavoidable emergency. Like a fool I would wait not knowing what to do. Without a nearby payphone I was stuck. If I left he would deride me. If I stayed there hungry and cold and scared, I hated myself. Anyone else with even a bit of self-respect would have drawn a boundary after the first time. Or at least arrange to meet at the destination or be picked up in a coffee shop. But I could not speak for fear I would be rejected. He liked how patient and accommodating I was, and I, being so starved for any kind of approval, did not have the heart not to do what he asked. And he always managed to make those evenings fun.

Besides the jazz clubs, I was introduced to other things, including steak tartare served in a European restaurant that years later he was bequeathed and managed to hang onto for a time.

And Scott, regular as clockwork, continued to torment me, calling me every six weeks or so. Now that he was married, any chance of a future with him was gone and I refused to see him. But I couldn't resist the phone calls and I knew this was taking a huge toll on my heart. I had to get serious about making a plan to put some major distance between us.

Chapter 16 - 1975

In January I got my Canadian Guild of Dispensing Opticians certification. I was determined to head west again as soon as possible and this would expand my work search options there. I was 20 years old and renting a room in my parents' house helped me to save money. I was still working at United Optical.

One day I had to deliver some lenses to Janice Roger who was the manager at the other store at 6351 Yonge St. in North York. I got there before they were open so I parked and stepped into the coffee shop next door to wait. At another table was a group of people my age, talking and laughing. One especially caught my eye: he was the spitting image of my 'teen' heartthrob, Jan Michael Vincent who starred in the 1972 movie "Sandcastles" which had had a great impact on me.

It's a story of how a car accident brings together a sensitive violinist and the ghost of the young man who is trying to remember why he can't leave the beach. They enjoy a doomed romance and building sandcastles while he figures out how to set a wrong right.

This movie had enchanted me so much that I couldn't get it out of my mind. The tenderness exhibited was what my teen fantasies were made of. The love shown in this movie was portrayed so well that it made me weep. It was so innocent and sweet, not like the movies we see today. It's unfortunate that many movies these days are way too focused on the sexiness aspects instead of the emotions that tug at the heartstrings. It's easy to forgive a film for the questions that it leaves you with when it touches your heart so deeply. Oh, to be 14 again and in love with a movie star!

I could not stop staring. Soon he noticed me and stared back with a playful smile. A few minutes later he came over, said hi and asked if I would join them. I was speechless. Before long, the two of us were having our own conversation. I learned his name was Roelof Hofman but everyone called him Dutchy as he was from Amsterdam. His father worked for the Canadian Embassy in Amsterdam and he had a brother there named John.

Dutch was an outgoing soul with a beautiful smile. People gravitated to him and he was thoughtful and loving to me. I could not believe that he paid me so much attention and that I had a chance.

I completed my errand while he waited and we drove back to town. I told him of my plan to move back to B.C. but needed to save enough money first. He said that he would like to come with me and we made a plan and shared it with Jurek, my cousin. Jurek had a dog, a beautiful silver german shepherd named Major that he could no longer keep. He asked if we could take him with us. Soon he was staying with me and would pick me up at the store each day.

Since Dutchy was working night security at some warehouse, he used my car to get to work, taking Major along on his rounds. By March we had saved enough for two plane fares and Major travelled in cargo for free. I was able to sell the car for extra cash.

Second move out west

Kelowna was even more beautiful than I remembered. A little town fronting an amazing lake, surrounded by orchards, while rolling hills silhouetted on the horizon. From what I had read, it was the #1 vacation spot in Canada. This is where everyone wanted to spend summer holidays. In my idealistic mind, our life choices were limitless, so why not just live there year round? But most of all, the scenery reminded me of my hometown in Poland: a small town on a river (as opposed to a lake) surrounded by gently rolling fields and hills.

We rented a room in an old hotel on Glenmore Street (now Gordon Drive) between Leon and Lawrence. We stayed there for two nights while we looked around for something more permanent. We found a cabin at a place called Blue Bird Resort at 4004 Lakeshore Road. It was right on the lake and we were very happy to move there. Dutch got a job at Kinney Shoes in Orchard Park Mall. I remember he bought a light denim three piece suit from Tip Top Tailors.

It was too early for fruit picking and since I abhorred the thought of any kind of sales job, I had a little more trouble finding work. I made a resume and posted notices on bulletin boards.

"Dear Sir or Madam,

My name is Isia Molin and I am a student optician with nine months experience. I would very much like to remain in this field and be able to continue my learning. If at present, (or in the future) you could use me, or know of someone who could, please give me a call at the above number. -

(resume inserted here)- I hope you will keep this letter on file and consider my application for any openings you may have. "

There were only two optical stores in town and there were no openings. There were also no reducing salons in Kelowna or apartments needing door viewers.

I finally got a call from a woman named Mrs. Powell who lived on Barkley Road in the Mission, who wanted help organizing her kitchen. I happily accepted, knowing that if I did a good job, I would have a local reference. There were no busses back then and Kelowna was a sleepy town with a population of perhaps 50,000 people, so we hitchhiked everywhere. The town was so small that the phone numbers were only 5 digits! Ours was 4-7051.

One of the places that intrigued me was Flintstones Bedrock Village so by April, I focused there. Unfortunately all the hiring had been done for the summer season but I was not discouraged. I went to see the manager Mrs. Sharoz every second day. I told her that I would take any job, even cleaning toilets. After a month she was finally impressed by my persistence and great attitude. Though she had no openings, I convinced her to give me a try for a week at no pay. She couldn't refuse. After three days, she hired me and put me in one of the concessions selling hotdogs and ice cream.

I was thrilled and sent Livia postcards. Soon I was promoted to work the till in the giftshop. In July, I sent Livia a postcard:

"It's about time I wrote! But since I work 6-7 days a week with only 1 day off, you can forgive me. It's a riot. I wear jeans or shorts and a Fred (Flintstone) t-shirt and there's about 50 kids 13-22 working here. Will write more soon. Love, Rini"

I made friends, the best one was Kathy whom I am still friends with 45 years later. (Among others were the Sandberg kids.)

Life was great. June was here and as the resort we were staying at was preparing for summer rentals at higher prices, we had to vacate. We were sad to leave our cosy piece of paradise where we were so happy, but it was too far to hitchhike each day anyway. We found a basement suite at 210 Woods Rd. in Rutland. We bought beautiful, durable sunset sheets at Sears, one of which I still have today. A young couple lived upstairs. The girl worked for the RCMP and they also had a dog.

We were now doing well enough to buy a car. Through his work contacts Dutch found a 1965 red Mustang coupe. All was working out for us except for one thing. He had migraines. Awful ones that would keep him in our darkened bedroom with complete silence for hours and me lonely, worried and unable to help him.

By September my summer job was ending and Dutch got a transfer to Vernon, and a position as assistant manager at Kinney's there. I was conflicted as life with him was just too sad for me.

The weekend of September 6-7th, we decided to give it one more try and set out on a road trip to Banff. On the way we stopped in Lake Louise for lunch. I sent Livia a postcard and we took some pictures. I got to pose on a horse. It was magical and I remember this trip as one of the happiest times of our relationship.

"Dear Liv, We're spending 2 days holidays here (Banff) and Lake Louise. It's beautiful driving and the weather is sunny but cool. We camped overnight and now we're headed back. Lots of luv, Rini"

"We must be willing to let go of the life we have planned, so as to have the life that is waiting for us" - E.M. Forster

Unfortunately a weekend of joy just wasn't enough. I preferred Kelowna and had little interest in moving to Vernon. But the key issue was that life with Dutchy consisted of him using up all his conversation and charm at work, then spending most evenings in bed with a migraine. It reminded me of my aunt Lidia. I needed someone to share good times with. Whether it was skiing or starting a family, more than anything, I wanted his presence. And evening after evening, lying next to him while he was in pain, just made me depressed.

I reflected on what else I would like to experience, and decided that travel while improving my French was a very attractive option. I found an au-pair agency and applied for a position in France. I cannot for the life of me remember how I did my research without the internet!

While I waited for a reply to my letter, Dutch helped me figure out the immediate logistics. We bought an old Valiant for $100 for me, and I rented a room at 735 Morrison Ave. He could not have been more supportive. He found a place to rent on an acreage and with our beautiful Mustang and our dog Major, Dutchy moved to Vernon.

The reference letter that I secured from Flintstones helped me to get the next job.

"To whom it may concern:

Dear Sirs;
This letter is to introduce Isia Molin who was employed as saleslady and cashier with Flintstones Bedrock City in Kelowna, B.C.

Isia was with us for a period of three months. We found her to be honest, reliable and courteous to customers, she was an extremely good worker and pleasant to work with.

I would highly recommend Isia as I know she would do justice to any position that she was given. Yours truly, Evelyn Szaroz, manager"

Waitressing at The Leper Colony

The Colony on Bernard Avenue was the hotspot in Kelowna; a great combination of restaurant, pizzeria and nightclub owned by Merv and Ann Lepper. Hence it was affectionately referred to as The Leper Colony!

I remember Merv as the best boss ever: he was fair, funny, generous, just and kind. And above all, competent. He ran a great place that all the staff and patrons loved. I remember how hard we worked and how he treated staff to drinks after closing and told us how well we did. The bartender was Frankie Johnson. He had a goatee and a wry sense of humour.

People came for the excellent pizza, for lunch, meetings, dinners, celebrations. The Corvette Club and the Orchard Country Ski Club had their meetings there. How great it was to have a place that had live bands, dinner and dancing in the evenings. People came to celebrate various special occasions, and no matter how they dressed, from graduation gowns to jeans, everybody was comfortable and fit in.

The Ye Olde Pizza Joint had a take out window onto Bernard St. as well as being open to the club. If the pizza order was wrong or singed, the staff got to eat it. About once a week at the end of the night, drinks were free. It was a wonderful place to work and had I been a better waitress, I would have likely stayed.

But I was not able to handle more than 4 tables at a time and I remember the kindest girl there was Debbie. She let me know when my orders were up and helped deliver them. I met members of the Orchard Country Ski Club who held their lunch meetings there. Also the Corvette Club and that's how I met Jack S. and Dale, my future dear friend

Darlene's brother. They all ribbed me good naturedly.

The room I rented on Morrison turned out to be my Flintstone's friend Kathy's childhood home. A blended family lived there and I felt very welcome. Kris Cline, the woman who owned the house, worked in the administration office of Capri Mall. Not sure what her boyfriend, David did. I occasionally babysat their daughter Aleisha who was approx. six years old. His son Daniel who was 17, occupied the other bedroom on the upper floor and had a motorcycle. I was very happy there, and I remember completing several macrame projects. Danny desperately wanted me, as the 'older' woman, to 'initiate' him but I was not interested.

Once again I wrote to Livia:

"Dear Livia,

So much has happened in the past weeks since I've been living here, I don't know where to start. I moved here to 735 Morrison at the end of August. The house is owned by the manager (Kris Cline) of one of the 2 shopping centers here, Capri, and she lives with her common-law husband David and her daughter Aleisha who is 6 years old. I've been pretty well accepted and do a lot of things with them.

Last week David's 17 year old son Danny moved in. So now I have an adopted brother (I adopted him yesterday mainly to keep him from getting any ideas or getting hung up on me or something.) He's really nice, going in for medicine at the college here (1st year), plays guitar, chess and rides a motorbike. As you can see we have a lot in common. He's also a Scorpio which I seem to get along with. So finally I can stop being jealous of you dear Livia, as I have a little kid sister and a younger brother, haha!

I took Aleisha to Flintstones once when I was working there and everybody thought she was either my sister or my kid. With a name that's similar to mine, (everybody calls me Isia here) she even looks like me.

I'm working at The Colony Steakhouse now that Flintstones is closed. I already miss it. I think it was the best job I've had so far. Anyway The Colony is the nicest place in Kelowna to go out and if I didn't get the job here, I wouldn't apply anywhere else for a waitress. It's not really my bag. But for now the boss is nice, the people are nice, the customers are nice and best of all the money's nice. I've paid off my (car) loan and am even saving money. I have to if I want to go (to France) in January. I haven't heard from the Greek Embassy yet, as I want to go first to Greece then to France; six months each.

I might even be in Toronto for Christmas. I just hope I don't get hooked on anybody before I leave. Cause if I don't go in January I'll never go. My 22nd birthday's in June and that's the end of youth fare. As long as I return before, it's only $430 return within a year ticket. Also in winter it's $100 less than the $530 in summer. After my birthday it goes on reg fare $900 return and I'll never be able to afford that.

Dutch is fine although I don't see him much. He wants to get back together, says he'll find me a job in Vernon but I just can't see it now. I'm happy living here, they're good to me, why should I go back to the bickering and fighting. He says he's changed, that now being on his own he sees how I am and what was wrong. But for some reason I've lost a lot of the feeling I had for him. And I've noticed that from just living here. That I don't really want to see him that often. We never even do anything. He never wants to. And you know how I used to run around doing anything and everything I could, signing up for yoga and dance and flying and going to Mosport etc. I miss that and I need it to feel *alive and to feel I'm not wasting my life standing still.*

Danny's teaching me to ride his motorbike, Christine and David have a sailboat, they also ski, so does Kathy (Dutch doesn't) (and I don't really feel like teaching him, I need to be taught. He doesn't even really want to learn. He'd probably just do it for me) and I'm already getting excited about skiing. Kathy is the girl I met at Flintstones, she's 18 and I think the only one I'll keep in touch with. She's a Gemini and it turns out she used to live in this house 3 years ago, and I'm living in her room!

I've been here almost 6 months now, and I guess it takes that long to settle, but now I feel like Kelowna's my home. I can't get enough of looking at the mountains and lake and when we went for a ride on Danny's bike yesterday, just going above the town and looking all around at it at your feet, it just still takes my breath away, although I've seen it at least 10 times.

I wake up in the morning with anticipation. I don't know how long this will last but I want to enjoy it while I can. Cause now I see that I've been down too long. And Dutch brings me down. I don't know whether he's getting too desperate or too hung up on me or what, but it's not good. He clutches, he tries to hold on so tight, I want to break loose or I'll lose myself.

In a way I'm disappointed it didn't work out, but then I learned so much from it, and that that's not enough for me. He just wants to get married. Period. What the hell am I gonna do then? Die? I think I would, he'd have me so tied. He wasn't like that before, I don't know whether I had that influence on him or what.

I love singing with the radio and I can't get enough of it now, even if it sounds worse than bad, I don't care. He always would put me down or turn the radio off. I guess we just don't have enough in common. But how do I tell him, I know he won't understand.

Anyway, enough of that! How's school, how's Ang, why don't you write?! Maybe I'll see you at Christmas (I'll come as long as I've got a ticket <u>out</u> of TO in my pocket!) but knowing us I'll probably need 2 months to catch up on everything!

Take care and keep happy, love Rini"

On my days off I would take the bus or drive down to visit my sister who still lived on Fleet Road off of Naramata Road. She had her hands full with her 20 month old son and picking fruit and canning. Sometimes an Australian boy named Phillip who worked there, gave me a ride back to Kelowna on his motorcycle. My favourite memory is of the several times that Basia and I went horseback riding either at the stables nearby or at Apex Mountain.

October came and went, I have a picture of me dressed up as a cavewoman for the Halloween shift. November came and my old Valiant would no longer start. I remember coming home one day and it was no longer parked out front. Cris told me she had it towed… her action wasn't unexpected. I had no money to fix it and there was no point in procrastinating. So hitchhiking became the norm again, save for an occasional ride home.

One of the customers caught my eye. Good looking though blond, his name was Terry and he was charming. He worked for Brian James at his ski store downtown on Lawrence. He was good looking, attentive and kind and I was soon smitten. He was living at the Mission Creek Motel and took me out on several dates. When I told him about my plans (hoping that he would talk me out of them), he never called again - which made the way even clearer for my departure.

Strange that I was still looking for a man to 'save' me from being independent, but when I had one that really wanted to marry me, I felt smothered and found fault in him… I started to realize that the problem in my relationships has been one of 'currency'.

Wrong currency

Parents who were not loving leave a huge hole in the heart of the child, that then she tries to fill in many ways. I grew up without hearing any loving words. Being a girl made me even more vulnerable to 'sweet talk'. What if someone gave me thousands of Russina 'rubles' or Chinese 'yuan' and I didn't appreciate it because it was of no value to me as I could not spend it? It might as well be monopoly money.

What quality in boys made me crave them or reject them? I decided to look for a pattern:

At age 12, Charlie expressed his adoration in writing. I longed for him for years.

At 14, Julek did in a song or two, but we never even shared a kiss.

At 16 I stopped dating Peter because though he was kind and generous, he was poor with words.

Lloyd was effusive in words and songs, but the religious issue was too strong.

At 17, Scott said all the right things to make my heart leap with joy each and every time I heard from him. Though there was no physical bonding, it was like a drink in the desert. The longing persisted throughout the years even without communication.

At 18, Chris led me in my best effort to deny the power of words.

At 19, Michael was the consummate salesman adept at manipulating with words. Though he had no other qualities that I desired, the words eventually ignited my emotions. Once the 'sweet talk' stopped, I had no trouble forgetting him.

At 20, Duchy was hard working and practical, yet I felt starved. He lacked the sweet talk.

Now with internet dating scams, older women make the biggest fools of themselves when they send some Nigerian sweet talker hundreds of thousands of dollars. And perhaps it's also one of the reasons women protect and return to abusive men who abuse to retain control… yet how much loyalty many women would give in exchange for a currency of loving words! Or ballroom dancing: but that's another story.

Near the end of November a band arrived from Toronto to perform at The Colony where I was working. The Great Rufus Road Machine, an up and coming band out of Ontario, consisted of husband and wife vocal team Russell and Sharon, Ken and John C. Baye on drums. They were in the process of making a name for themselves and were a big hit in small town Kelowna. The restaurant was packed each of the 5 days they played and I was exhausted trying to keep up with the dinner orders. After closing, the staff and band relaxed together. There was no sign of drugs of any kind. After their gig was done, they played several days in Penticton at the Three Gables Tavern. While there, John who was the drummer, wrote me poetry. But that didn't impress me as it was lacking in sweet talk. After Penticton they were driving back to Toronto. I was even more impatient to leave and took this as a sign. For $40 dollars towards gas, I had my ride. They had a van and a truck so having a 6th person along helped them as well. A driver and a navigator for each vehicle while 2 slept, meant the trip could be made in as short a time as possible. There were no gigs scheduled on the way back, so we made it to Toronto in four days.

I was able to store a couple of boxes of my possessions at my Flintstone friend Kathy's mom's house. My guitar, my music books and most of my clothes were coming with me. We left on December 4th and apart from tons of snow coming down along the way, the drive was pretty much uneventful. What stands out most for me was that John slept with his eyes open and being a black belt in martial arts, he could hit a stop sign with a snowball from quite a distance away.

Back in Toronto

I arrived at the house on Indian Rd. Cresc. where my parents now lived. My father was busy renovating; tearing out walls to give it a more modern open plan. I wasn't keen to spend too much time in Toronto, but as I had saved only enough money for my round trip to Europe ticket, Greece was out as a first stop as I had no contacts or job there. Soon I received a letter from the au-pair agency that they had a posting for me and would advise me soon. So it was just a matter of waiting now.

I went to find a job for some extra cash. This time I got hired as a waitress at CN's (Canadian National Railways) newest restaurant, which consisted of converted railroad cars. After a week, much to the disapproval of the other waitresses, and I suspect based mostly on my accommodating attitude and youth, I was promoted to hostess.

I did not see Michael. There was nothing he could help me with and I did not want my decision to be questioned or contradicted. I did not hear back from the Greek Embassy. My interest in going there was not about Chris, but because of how my sister raved about it. Plus I loved learning languages and wanted to improve my Greek. I could read it easily, but wanted an opportunity to practice speaking it.

I did spend some much needed catchup time with Livia though, and called Lloyd as well. He still thought that he and I belonged together. How sad that he seemed to feel for me the way that I felt for Scott.

He told me that the 1973 Edward Bear song described too well his feelings for me.

"I dreamed she came back home last night

Asked her where she'd been

She said I've been around the world and

It almost did me in

She said I hope you didn't wait too long

I had no sense of time

I see you've written one Last Song

And I realized it's mine

Think of all the times we talked

Sing a nursery rhyme.

Close your eyes

I'm right beside you

Run for miles you know I'll find you

Cause it's all the same

Change your lovers

Change your name

If you need a friend

Close your eyes

I'm back again.

She really came back home last night

Seemed as if she'd changed

Said that she'd go back to school

And try things once again

But you know it didn't take too long

Till she lost her way

And all the reason in the world could see

She couldn't stay

As I helped her pack her things"

His voice could have doubled for the lead singer of that band and anytime I hear any of their songs, I cannot help but say a little prayer for Lloyd.

He also told me he'd been busy writing songs but his life at home was complicated. Being 20 years old now, his father was pressuring him to 'grow up' by giving up his dream of being a musician and going to work for him at Southam Publishing where he was the president of the company and a very wealthy man. Recently the pressure had turned to threats: "if you don't do as I say, I will disown you and leave you penniless".

In my naivete that anything you set your mind to is possible, I encouraged him to call his father's bluff. Sadly that did not turn out as well for him as it had for me. I found out just how much stronger I was...

Chapter 17 - 1976

Several days later in January, I received a letter advising me of my placement as a 'governess'. After purchasing a one year student return ticket to Europe and writing to my host family, it felt safe to call Scott just to say 'hi' and 'bye'.

He told me that he was driving for Trimac Transport, delivering cement bags. And that his wife of less than two years had left him. He couldn't wait to see me. And I could no longer say no. He worked days and I worked evenings, so it wasn't easy, but we finally managed to spend many happy hours together. Yet, he was torn once again so my leaving made it easy for him. Sometimes the purpose of relationships is simply to complete unfinished business from a past life, I reasoned.

At work, since I had been a poor waitress and had no seniority, the waitresses resented my being in charge of their table assignments. So they found a way to oust me. One evening Tony the assistant manager asked me into his office to total the day's receipts and closed the door. Nothing happened but the next day I was let go with no explanation. I didn't care: to me, jobs were easy to find. And anyway, I was on my way to France!

Somehow I never lacked for initiative or courage to make a change or pursue a dream. Even if my choices were not well thought out as in this instance: I disliked big cities and had specifically asked for a small town and hence the delay as most of the requests for au pairs came from Paris for the homes of well off people like doctors, lawyers and government officials. So at the end of January, I was on my way to the industrial city of Mulhouse.

Scott offered to take me to the airport and Livia insisted on coming as well. We had an awkward farewell as we were both self conscious with expressing our feelings in front of Livia. I hadn't had a chance to fill her in on my time with him and I was sure she would have disapproved.

I set off for this new and exciting adventure. I boarded the plane and settled into my window seat on the right side. As we lined up on the runway for takeoff, I looked out the window to have one last look at snowy Toronto. Imagine my surprise, when on the roof of the round parkade, I saw a single car with a man standing on the roof of the Camaro, waving his arms like mad! What an incredibly memorable send off. I smiled all the way to Paris.

First month in Mulhouse

With my guitar case, suitcase and a carry on bag, I landed at Orly Airport in Paris and found my way to the railway station where I exchanged some money (4 francs to a dollar) and bought a ticket for Mulhouse. I sent a telegram to my host family advising them of my scheduled arrival. Some three hours later, I was there. I remember it was evening and getting dark. People came and went and soon the train station was nearly empty and still no sign of my ride. I found a payphone and called. The woman who answered the phone told me that they did not live far and gave me directions to reach the house. Not a good sign!

This wasn't exactly the welcome that I had hoped for, but once I arrived, I found the couple to be polite though a bit standoffish. The children were already in bed. I was shown a room that belonged to their apartment but was on the fourth floor. The attic had a row of 'servant' rooms with a lavatory for all to share. Some were occupied by students and a couple by elderly women, possibly relatives of other tenants. Several were vacant. Each small room contained a small window under the eaves, a single bed, a desk and chair and a sink and mirror. The family lived in an apartment on the second. Great, I thought, my own space. As I settled down to sleep, I noticed 'tally marks' where a past occupant had kept track of their days there… I turned out the light.

The next morning I joined the household for breakfast. A nice looking, average French couple where the husband had a job and the wife was a stay at home mom. Their daughter Marina age 3 ½ took after her mom with her personality and dark hair. Daniel, age 2, was the image of his blond father. They were to be my full time responsibility as the mom was eager to find a job. It only took a couple of days for them to trust me. Apart from dressing and feeding them I took them for walks and to the nearby park. Unfortunately with both parents gone most days of the week, I had little chance to practise my french. Soon a solution presented itself: in my free time, as I explored the town, I came across a notice advertising french evening classes for 'new citizens' offered twice a week at a nearby school.

My first evening in class introduced me to around 15 or so students of all ages and races while chief among them stood out my new best friend Lisette Holbek from Denmark. She was younger than I, blond and gorgeous. Whenever our teacher gave instructions, she would mumble "Bloody hell" in a very British accent. I first reacted with shock and then laughter. On subsequent evenings she proceeded to smoke a cigar in class while pointing to the 'no cigarette smoking' sign when the teacher objected.

She was also an au-pair and we became fast friends spending Sundays, our days off, together. A bit of a terror on her scooter, she would come into town to pick me up and take me to Illzach - a little village just four kilometres north of Mulhouse where she lived with her host family. They were usually out of town on Sundays and she would serve me a hilarious version of formal afternoon British tea. Tablecloth, fine china, baby finger raised and all.

Since she had already been there several months, she also introduced me to her friends who then showed me where I could connect with the Polish community. It wasn't long and I was attending a Polish folk dancing class.

Yet I hesitated to sign the six month minimum contract with the family as things weren't turning out as well for me as they were for them. Within a month, I was being given more and more responsibilities. Though the mother didn't work, she made a point of being out a lot. And when she was home, she made no attempt at conversation apart from barking commands at me and sending me to run errands and do the daily shopping. I didn't mind this as it gave me a chance for some real life conversations to practice my French, but with a high percentage of the population from Algeria, it was a bit scary as many tended to lack in civilized behavior.

I soon realized that I had made a huge mistake not choosing Paris. This one income family could hardly afford me, yet the wife carried on as if she was some grand lady who only spoke to me out of necessity. I felt like I was some 19th century servant expected to be grateful that she had graced me with employment.

The more competent I showed myself to be, the more work I was assigned and soon my 'governess' responsibilities morphed into domestic for the same pay. As I was put in charge of the laundry and cleaning, it left me less and less time to tend to the toddlers. And since my first priority was to improve my french, I started to feel that I was brought there under false pretenses. Yet I didn't know how to speak up for myself and object.

My day started at 7a.m. feeding the children and cleaning the kitchen after breakfast. Then off to town to shop. Afterwards, whether the mother was home or not, I had to run the laundry and deal with a stack of ironing which included cotton sheets. Even in Poland no one ironed sheets! Then feed the kids lunch, put them down for a nap and vacuum the floors or wash the windows. This included the sweeping and washing of the 2nd floor landing as well as the full set of stone stairs between the first and second floor. The parents made dinner while I tended to the kids' baths. We usually ate around 6 and it was left to me to clean up while the family retired to the living room. At first the husband who was kind and meek, would roll up his sleeves to wash dishes and converse with me, but that did not last long. His wife made it clear that that was unacceptable to her. On days that I didn't have class or dance, I was expected to help until 7 or 8 p.m. when I headed upstairs and played guitar late into the night. Songs full of sorrow and longing.

Now I understood the 'tally marks' on the wall, but I was still determined to make the best of it.

Second month

Another month passed by and one day the teacher advised us that there was going to be a strike and french language classes were being suspended. That was a big disappointment, but I was still able to hang onto my good humour by attending the

Polish club and spending most Sundays with Lisette. And responding to letters from Scott. Until one day he informed me that his wife came back and they were giving their marriage another chance.

On March 12th, I sent Livia a postcard:

"Salut!

Ca va bien? Il faut que j'écris au moins un fois en français. Nous sommes sortis avec un avocat mercredi soir, et le reste du temps je reste à la maison parce qu'il y a un grève à l'école. Et maintenant je vais à Illzach chez mon amie Lisa. Au revoir, love, Rini."

("Hi!

Things are going well? I have to write at least once in French. We went out with a lawyer on Wednesday night, and the rest of the time I stay at home because there is a school strike. And now I'm going to Illzach with my friend Lisa. see you,")

I met some of the family's friends and one Sunday, a couple with a lovely 6 year old daughter invited me to come for tea. They confided that they heard how hard I worked and would love for me to have a more reasonable living arrangement with them, but could not risk offending their friends by making me that offer. Another friend that my host family introduced me to, was a young attorney who upon leaving post visit, asked to take me out for dinner. I was happy to accept. Several days later he picked me up with flowers in hand and took me to a lovely restaurant. I got a very cold reception from the children's mother the next day. She rebuked me and shamed me. My date did not call again.

I entertained myself with music. I bought a cassette of Maxine Le Forrestier and improved my french by memorizing several of his songs.

Third month

Just as I was considering making a change, the wife sat me down and informed me that they were planning to drive to 'Les Gets' for a ski holiday and I needed to purchase insurance. I refused, saying that according to the contract, the host family was responsible for my insurance. She reminded me that since I still had not signed the contract, the cost fell to me. Though I was already thinking and dreaming in French, I was missing much vocabulary for these kinds of discussions.

I took stock of my situation. I was making the equivalent of $75 per month (plus room and board) for 72-75 hours of hard work each week. I compared that to the $300 a month for a 40 hour work week that I had been clearing at Procter and Gamble two years earlier.

This just did not feel good, and so the next day I hesitantly told her I could not afford the insurance and therefore would not go. That changed her mind as a ski trip with two toddlers would not allow her much time to ski. She relented and a week later we left.

Les Gets Ski Resort is located in southern France, between Lake Geneva and Mont Blanc, sharing its slopes with Morzine. To get there, we drove most of the 300 km through Switzerland.

We stayed in a 'pensionat' (a self catered apartment in a private house) for 7-8 days and cooked our own meals. The weather was great and the parents were happy skiing while I spent the days playing with the children inside and outside. They were so happy in fact, that the day before we left, they allowed me half a day to ski. I was thrilled and enjoyed it immensely. So happy in fact, that I just had to purchase a Les Gets souvenir: my first patch to sew onto my canvas bag. (which being overly sentimental, I still have, haha!)

Back in Mulhouse, I noticed the parents were bickering more and more. The husband was meek up till now, but even he had enough of his unreasonable bossy wife. It was clear to me that it was time to leave. Imagine my shock when upon giving my notice, the wife starts speaking perfect English! She was now determined to change my mind but it was too little too late. I refused to sign the contract which would have granted me the ability to stay longer than three months.

My dysfunctional upbringing and my outdated coping mechanisms had sabotaged my dreams at each crossroads.

Life is a constant process of letting go

And so after three months, another change was in the works. Somehow in my short life, I had managed to develop the attitude that nothing ventured meant nothing gained. And failing meant that I was to perhaps try doing things a different way. And to always have a plan B.

Though I originally planned to spend a few months in Greece as well as France, after three months in a crappy industrial town in France with such low pay that even though I saved what I could, I only had enough money for a train ticket to either Greece or Poland. Not both. Homesickness won. I explored the train schedules and bought a ticket for Poznań, Poland.

The journey of around 15-18 hours took me to France's main train hub of Metz, where I changed to a train that would take me through West Germany, then East Germany and on to the city of Poznań where I walked into town to exchange some money so that I could buy a ticket to Cieszyn. In no less than five minutes, I was approached by a friendly looking man who asked me if I was looking for a currency exchange. When I said yes, he made it very easy for me by pulling out a wad of Polish currency. The going rate was 100 to 1, meaning I got a 100 zloty for 1 Canadian dollar. Happy to have accomplished my first goal, I failed to realize that I had also committed my first crime, as exchanging currency on the black market was grounds for arrest.

Fortunately I was spared the consequences and was soon on a steam driven train heading for my hometown. Everything so far was how I left it. I selected a compartment that I was still so familiar with and took a seat on the second class wooden bench.

I remember there was a man in the compartment who was very vocal about the ironies of the communist government. He gave examples such as "it's legal to buy things using dollars, while it is illegal to possess foreign currency. There was no unemployment but there were many people with nothing to do." He said there was a black market book written with great humor on the subject. I told him I was interested in that book and realized my mistake when I saw the looks of horror on the faces of the other occupants. That was my second lesson: don't say, read or even listen to anything that did not show the rulers in a positive light. Guardian angels protected me once more. This was 13 years before the Iron curtain fell, and the communist government was still firmly in power, supported by the USSR with their military might just in case it was needed.

I couldn't believe my eyes when the train finally pulled into the bustling Cieszyn station that had been built in 1869. It was just as I remembered it 12 years earlier. And just as it was in my grandmother's youth.

I was sure that I was dreaming. I could hardly contain my joy: Communism or not, poverty or not, I was finally back in my much missed and much loved hometown, coming full circle back to where my life began.

And blissfully unaware that I would be ushered out again with just a little bit more warning than when I was ten...

Made in the USA
Monee, IL
23 November 2020